Infinite Circle

Infinite Circle

TEACHINGS IN ZEN

BERNIE GLASSMAN

SHAMBHALA
BOSTON & LONDON
2003

Shambhala Publications, Inc.
Horticultural Hall
300 Massachusetts Avenue
Boston, Massachusetts 02115
www.shambhala.com

Printed in the United States of America

✑ This edition is printed on acid-free paper that meets the
American National Standards Institute z39.48 Standard.
♻ Shambhala Publications makes every effort to print on recycled
paper. For more information please visit www.shambhala.com.

Distributed in the United States by Random House, Inc.,
and in Canada by Random House of Canada Ltd

Library of Congress Catalogues the hardcover edition
of this book as follows:

Glassman, Bernard (Bernard Tetsugen)
Infinite circle: teachings in Zen / Bernie Glassman
p. cm.
ISBN 978-1-59062-591-6 (cloth)
ISBN 978-1-59030-079-4 (paperback)
1. Zen Buddhism—Doctrines. 2. Spiritual Life—Zen
Buddhism. 3. Tripiṭaka. Sūtrapiṭaka. Prajñāpāramitā. Hṛdaya—
Criticism and interpretation. I. Title.
BQ9265.4.G53 2002   294.3'420427—dc21   2001049069

Contents

Acknowledgments

My warmest gratitude and appreciation go to Sensei Lou Mitsunen Nordstrom, who took my discursive, meandering talks and pulled them together into a single, cohesive manuscript; to Sensei Eve Myonen Marko, who edited the manuscript for publication; and to my students at the Zen Community of New York, who not only transcribed the talks but also asked the questions.

Introduction

Think of not-thinking. How do you think of not-thinking? Non-thinking. This in itself is the essential art of zazen [Zen meditation]. Zazen is not learning meditation. It is simply the Dharma-gate of repose and bliss, the practice-realization of totally culminated enlightenment. It is the manifestation of ultimate reality. Traps and snares can never reach it. Once its heart is grasped, you are like the dragon when he gains the water, like the tiger when he enters the mountain. For you must know that right there, in zazen, the right Dharma is manifesting itself and that, from the first, dullness and distraction are struck aside.

—Dogen Zenji

In this book I will attempt to clarify these words[1] of Dogen Zenji, the founder of the Japanese Soto Zen sect, whose writings I first encountered in 1968 when I read his essay, "Being Time." At that time I was completing my studies for a doctorate in applied mathematics and was struck by Dogen's descrip-

---

1. Norman Waddell and Masao Abe, trans., "Fukanzazengi (The Universal Promotion of the Principles of Zazen) by Dogen Zenji," in *On Zen Practice II: Body, Breath and Mind*, ed. Hakuyu Taizan Maezumi and Bernard Tetsugen Glassman (Los Angeles: Zen Center of Los Angeles, 1976).

tion of space and time. Here was a thirteenth-century thinker writing about concepts we were just starting to develop in modern physics and mathematics! Not long thereafter I was fortunate enough to begin my studies with my teacher, Taizan Maezumi Roshi, under whose guidance I began to explore the world that Dogen Zenji had described.

Dogen Zenji says that zazen, or Zen meditation, is the actualization of the Enlightened Way. Zazen is not simply a technique to learn to become enlightened or to learn to calm the mind or to strengthen the body. Zazen *is* the Enlightened Way. The simplest form of zazen is sitting meditation. But it goes far beyond that. As Shakyamuni Buddha said, "Everything as it is, is the Enlightened Way!" Thus zazen is the thunder, the lightning, the rain. Zazen is the elimination of distance between subject and object. But what is zazen? What is enlightenment? What is actualization? I hope the following chapters will help clarify these terms for you.

This book is based on a series of three workshops I offered at the Greyston Seminary of the Zen Community of New York in Riverdale, New York, on the *Heart Sutra, The Identity of Relative and Absolute* (the eighth-century poem by Ch'an Master Shih-t'ou Hsi-ch'ien), and the Bodhisattva Precepts. The three studies together parallel the structure of koan study, developed by eighteenth-century Zen teacher Hakuin Ekaku in Japan. Koan study is traditionally practiced in face-to-face encounters between student and teacher and requires an experiential, rather than an intellectual, grasp of the material. So please read this text as if we were talking to each other, as indeed we are. Using the *Heart Sutra* text, we will explore the intimacies of Zen practice and leap into the realm of not-thinking, or not-knowing. We will then penetrate into Dogen's world of practice-realization by discussing *The Identity of Relative and Absolute.* Finally, we will broaden our perspective by analyzing the Bodhisattva Precepts (or *Kai,* "aspects of our life") that constitute the Right Dharma.

These workshops were given in the early years of the Zen Community of New York. We had developed a strong meditation practice and study program and were just beginning our social action ministry. Ahead of us was the move to southwest Yonkers and the development—over a period of some fifteen years—of the Greyston model for social change, informed by Buddhist values and vibrantly alive and thriving to this very day. Ahead of me was the founding of the Zen Peacemaker Order and the beginnings of the Peacemaker Community, open to peacemakers of all spiritual persuasions who wish to integrate their practice with social activism.

So why do I now publish a book about the *Heart Sutra,* which talks of the emptiness of the elements that make up human nature, or about a poem describing in rigorous detail the complex relationship between the relative and absolute realms? Why is this compulsory study for members of the Zen Peacemaker Order alongside trainings in social ministry, liturgy, and nonviolence?

In Zen, there are two ways of describing reality. Basically, one says that reality is all One, that everything is Buddha. The other describes the manyness of reality, its multitude of diverse phenomena and differences. What both sutras say is that these two ways of perceiving reality are not just valid, but essentially the same. Over the years, Zen masters have developed practices to help us see reality first from both sides separately and then from both as an equivalence.

As I've become more and more involved in social action, I see the issue of oneness and diversity not only as a primary issue in Zen practice, but perhaps as *the* issue in the peacemaking world. I see this in the many places around the globe where systematic massacres and widespread ethnic cleansing are predicated on the notion that there's only one way to be, one way to behave, one God to believe in, and that all else is somehow invalid. There are always some things that we exclude from the One, that we can't possibly believe are enlightened as they are, that we can't believe are *it*. This points to the importance of prajna wisdom, to not seeing things in a dualistic, inside/outside way but rather experiencing the vibrancy of everything as it is, at this very moment.

On the other hand, we are often tempted to sit and not do. For years I encountered Zen practitioners who felt that until they were fully enlightened there was no use acting in the world; they would simply be acting out of delusion. I have argued forcefully that we have to act. We don't practice in order to attain enlightenment; because we are enlightened, we practice. In the same way, we don't act in the world in order to make everything One; because we are One, we act! Bodhisattvas don't vow to work forever simply to attain results or objectives that are exterior to themselves. Because they are prajnaparamita, because they embody the wisdom that everything is interconnected without exception, they strive to save all beings. The more clearly we see this, the more appropriately we act. In fact, we have no choice in the matter.

For me, practice has always been about the One Body. Not just the One Body as a single entity, as One, but also as a million billion different components and pieces, each of which is the One Body. I would say that the great quest from time immemorial has not been the search for or even the realization of Oneness—that seems to have existed from early on—but rather the honoring of each particular, each individual aspect of the One Body as the One Body itself, without excluding something or someone, without mandating that all things be a particular way in order to be part of that One Body.

As our leaders are fond of reminding us, we now live in a

global community. It's interesting to me that in the political, economic, and scientific spheres, synonyms for the One Body are being developed every day: globalization, common markets, one world economy, the Internet. And immediately the same issue arises: Can this move toward globalization, towards recognizing that we're all One, allow for the equal importance of diverse cultures, economies, traditions, and needs? Can we honor each component as the One Body rather than honoring the One Body at the expense of its components? This has always been humanity's great challenge, and it's equally the great challenge facing peacemakers today.

The third section of this book discusses the Bodhisattva Precepts according to the Japanese Soto Zen sect, focusing on the Three Treasures, the Three Pure Precepts, and the first Grave Precept, Nonkilling. I included this discussion because it asks the question, how do we know what is the appropriate action to take at any given moment? In the Zen Peacemaker Order, we've formulated the precepts in a somewhat different manner (in the Epilogue I describe some of these changes and the reasons behind them), but the question of what to do and how best to do it is a living question for all of us. By that I mean that there is no one answer. Whatever answer exists is situational, arising and disappearing with the circumstances. Ultimately there is nothing to do other than act out of non-separation and bear witness. There is nothing to rely on, only the rich unfolding of life and our fearless, spontaneous response to it, moment by moment.

BERNIE GLASSMAN
Santa Barbara, Easter 2001

The Heart of the Perfection of Great Wisdom Sutra

The Heart of the Perfection
of Great Wisdom Sutra

Avalokitesvara Bodhisattva doing deep prajnaparamita
Perceived the emptiness of all five conditions
And was freed of pain.
O Shariputra, form is no other than emptiness,
Emptiness no other than form;
Form is precisely emptiness,
Emptiness precisely form.
Sensation, perception, reaction, and consciousness are also
    like this.
O Shariputra, all things are expressions of emptiness:
Not born, not destroyed; not stained, not pure; neither
    waxing nor waning.
Thus emptiness is not form,
Not sensation nor perception, reaction nor consciousness;
No eye, ear, nose, tongue, body, mind;
No color, sound, smell, taste, touch, thing;
No realm of sight, no realm of consciousness;
No ignorance, no end to ignorance;
No old age and death, no cessation of old age and death;
No suffering, no cause or end to suffering;
No path, no wisdom, and no gain.
No gain—thus Bodhisattvas live this prajnaparamita
With no hindrance of mind.

No hindrance, therefore no fear.
Far beyond all such delusion, Nirvana is already here.
All past, present, and future buddhas live this prajnaparamita
And attain supreme, perfect enlightenment.
Therefore know that prajna paramita is the holy mantra,
The luminous mantra, the supreme mantra, the
    incomparable mantra
By which all suffering is cleared.
This is no other than truth.
Therefore, set forth the prajnaparamita mantra,
Set forth this mantra and proclaim:
Gate, gate, paragate, parasamgate, bodhi svaha!

1
No Yellow Brick Road

The Heart of the Perfection of Great Wisdom Sutra
Maha Prajnaparamita Hrdaya Sutra

The Wisdom literature, or the Prajnaparamita sutras, exists in many different lengths. There are versions of one hundred thousand, twenty-five thousand, eight thousand, one hundred, and fifty lines. The version I'm discussing here is twenty-four lines and represents the heart (*hrdaya*), or essence, of the Prajnaparamita.

Some people say it's not necessary to read the *Heart Sutra* in its English translation, that the essence of this Wisdom literature can be achieved by just chanting it in the original Sanskrit. Before I review the meaning of the title, let me say that when you truly *just* chant the *Heart Sutra,* all of it is contained in the act of just chanting. When we chant in such a way that nothing else is happening, that all our concentration, all our mental and physical energies are condensed into just being the sound *A* (the first syllable of the original text, from "Avalokitesvara"), that is all that exists. Just A! Just the elimination of any trace of separation between subject and object, which is nothing but our zazen itself. If we put all our energy into just chanting in

5

this manner, there is no separation, and that state of no separation is the state of *sunyata,* or "emptiness," or what I also call not-knowing. That is the state of 100 percent action; everything is fully concentrated in this very moment. This is the heart of our practice, to be totally in this moment, moment after moment. It doesn't matter what words are being chanted; when you are totally *A,* it is not even *A* anymore; it is the whole universe, it is everything.

This is the essence of the first word of the Sanskrit title of the *Heart Sutra*: *Maha.* The entire title in Sanskrit is *Maha Prajnaparamita Hrdaya Sutra,* or in English, *The Heart of the Perfection of Great Wisdom Sutra.* In a way, the whole text—as well as all of Zen teaching—is summed up in this title.

Maha is commonly translated as "great" in both a quantitative and qualitative sense—in fact in a very special sense. Maha is so great that there is no outside. An analogy from mathematics may help. If you draw a circle, that circle includes certain things and excludes certain things. If you make a larger circle, there are still going to be things outside the circle. In mathematics, one way of defining a circle or determining its size is by trying to find something outside it. You ask of any given object, "Is this inside or outside?" If it's outside, then you know the object is exterior to the circle.

Let's look at ourselves. I draw a circle representing who I think I am. In a way, we all do that. When I say that maha means there's no outside, then any object I name is inside the circle of myself, of who I think I am. Everything is nothing but me. If I look at anger, that's me; it's not outside me. If I look at the trees and the river, they're me, too; they're not outside me. Everybody reading this book is me. Moreover, the stars and moon are me; they're not outside. If this is true, then each one of us is this maha. If we are all within the same circle, then all of this is One Body; there is no outside. Since there is no outside, there is no inside either. This is one of the major teachings of Buddhism and one of the fundamental teachings of Zen.

When we introduce the term *outside,* that automatically introduces the correlative term *inside* and creates a boundary, a circle. If there is no outside—for the circle is infinite—then not only is there no inside, there is also no circle anymore. What remains is a single entity, just one thing. This is what is meant by One Body, which is the fundamental meaning of maha.

Maha is all-inclusive, nothing is left out. In this sense maha also describes what's known as the Way (*Tao*). Since maha is no-outside-and-no-inside, it is therefore the Way. By contrast, people tend to think that the Way is some kind of path, or that it refers to *the* way of doing things or some sort of direction that we take. But the Tao is everything. Each of us is the Way; each of us is walking the Way.

You remember Dorothy from *The Wizard of Oz?* Someone sets her on the yellow brick road so that she will finally get to the Wizard of Oz. But there is no yellow brick road! We are already on it. Wherever we are, that is the yellow brick road, that's the Tao, that's maha. And maha declares that there is no outside or inside to the path. Everything is the path; we are all on the Way. Where? It doesn't go anywhere! It's the pulsating of life everywhere.

The second word in the title is *Prajna,* which is usually translated in English as "wisdom," but in a special sense. In some meditation halls, a monitor hits the shoulders of the meditators with an encouraging stick known as the sword of wisdom, or Manjusri's sword, to help cut off their delusions during meditation, to cut away all their ideas and notions. So this prajna is not wisdom in the sense of knowledge or a gathering of information, nor does it refer to an omniscient sage who knows all the answers. It's not even the wisdom implied in understanding the essence of life. We speak of prajna as the wisdom of emptiness.

Prajna is empty in the sense that it has no content of its own. It's nothing but the functioning of maha, which is the One Body, or everything as it is. It's the functioning of reality at this very moment, of nothing but this very moment. Being hot, we sweat; the very act is prajna. Sweating is the wisdom of being hot because it's the functioning of this moment as being hot. You light a candle and the light itself is prajna. When we walk in the rain, we get wet—that's prajna. We step on a dog turd and our shoe stinks—that's prajna, the functioning of what is.

A Nazi putting a young child into the Auschwitz gas chamber is also prajna, so we can't look at prajna in terms of right and wrong, good and bad. The sword of Manjusri, the sword of wisdom, cuts away all dualisms, leaving only what is. The functioning of that state is prajna. It's so vast that most of the time we don't realize we're even experiencing it. For example, you are experiencing a leaf falling from a tree somewhere in Connecticut right now, even though you don't realize it. That's prajna. It's the sounds that we hear, the rain, the sunlight, the smell of flowers, the airplane overhead—directly experienced as not being separate from us. When our ideas or concepts drop away, so does the separation from what is, and the very functioning of this nonseparation is what we mean by prajna. Because prajna is the functioning of maha and maha is nothing but us, prajna is our functioning and we are nothing but prajna.

The first half of the *Heart Sutra* explains what this prajna is. The second half explains the functioning of the bodhisattvas, those who realize this prajna. We all manifest prajna, but bodhisattvas have a realization of what it is. It turns out that we are bodhisattvas too, as we shall soon see.

The next word in the title is *paramita,* which is often translated as "perfection." However, *param* literally means "to go to the other shore." Paramita is the present perfect tense ("having gone to the other shore"), so it means "at the other shore." Do you know where the other shore is? Some people call the other shore nirvana. Being at the other shore thus means that nirvana is already here. It signifies that we have already gotten to the place where we are this One Body. Instead of thinking of going from the state of delusion to the state of enlightenment, what paramita means is that we are already there. *This* is the other shore; *this* is the state of enlightenment.

We talk about six paramitas, of which prajnaparamita is only one. But the *Heart Sutra* deals with prajna as the vehicle that takes us where we already are—this is it! Now obviously, if everything is nothing but the One Body, how could there be another shore? On the other hand, if this was so clear to us we'd have no need for Manjusri's sword cutting off the delusion of duality. But we do! For although there is no other shore, it is neither obvious nor acceptable to us. We are always searching for that other shore, for something extra, something outside ourselves, thinking it is some wonderful place we are going to find. We refuse to accept the fact that this is it.

We don't go to the other shore; the other shore comes to us. Something happens, and we awaken to the realization that under our feet lies the shoreline. This very body is the Buddha, and all the sounds of the world—everything that happens as is—are the Buddha's teachings.

Everything in Zen is present perfect tense. There is no future, no past—it's all now. There's nowhere to go, nowhere to reach, it's all here, all One Body, one thing. Since we are already here, we are already at the end of the path and we are also at the beginning. We don't practice to become enlightened, we don't practice to realize something; we practice *because* we are enlightened. We don't eat to live; *because* we are alive, we eat. We usually think it's the other way around, that we eat and breathe so we'll be or remain alive. But no because we're alive, we breathe, we eat, we do.

To say that we practice to realize the Way misses the point, because it implies that through practice we're going to attain something, maybe enlightenment. That same logic implies that because we breathe, we're going to be alive, as if being alive results from breathing. No, both are happening at the same time. They're not linear; cause and effect are one.

We generally tend to look at life from a linear perspective: We do something and that causes something else to happen later. But in fact it's all happening at this very moment. There seems to be a linear sequence, but it's not real. Looking at a movie, we think it's continuous, but in fact it's composed of separate frames. Reality—everything—is here right now. Our minds think that what happens this moment is going to create the next moment, and in a way it does, but this way of seeing things is misleading. Both what happens now and what happens later are all here right now, this very moment.

If we stop breathing, of course, we won't live very long. Because breathing is the very function of life, one can't not breathe. But breathing doesn't cause life, it's inseparable from it. Breathing *is* life. It can no more be separated from life than wetness from water. The oneness of cause and effect is this complete inseparability.

Dogen Zenji says that firewood does not become ash. From our linear viewpoint, we think that the burning of firewood causes the firewood to become ash. But there is no such thing as becoming! Firewood is firewood and functions as firewood; ash is ash and functions as ash. Breathing is life, life is breathing; they're not related as cause and effect. Just as firewood does not become ash, so life does not become death. Life is life and functions completely as life. Death is death and functions completely as death.

To say there is no such thing as becoming follows from the fact that this is all One Body, all one thing. It does *not* mean that things don't change. Shakyamuni Buddha said that everything is change. This is it—and it's changing. This is the enlightened state and it's changing. If we can really see that, if we can really let it soak in, there is no way to be upset about ourselves, no way to feel dissatisfied or guilty about not doing things right. It's all going to change, whatever it is. Instead of being tormented by guilt and bad feeling, we simply say, "Well, let's do it better." Whatever *it* is, is the enlightened state.

Since this is the enlightened state, it is the best that could happen at this very moment—but best in the special sense that it's happening and there is no choice. It is in this sense that we say everything is perfect just as it is, in the sense of being complete. Take an incense bowl. It's perfect as it is. If I drop it and it breaks into a lot of pieces, each piece is perfect as it is—because that's what it is. We may have the notion that all those pieces should be returned to their original condition as parts of a whole incense bowl so they can be perfect again, but that's just a notion.

Another synonym for perfect is *absolute*. The pieces are just what they are. If we add anything to the incense bowl, we don't make it more perfect, we change it to something different. We are perfect as we are. If we add another head on top of our own, we create something else, another kind of creature. If we add anything to who we are, we're something different. Therefore, whatever happens at any given moment is the best that could happen at that moment. Any other conclusion is the result of our ideas about how things should be or are supposed to be, and these too are just notions.

Sometimes it helps to think of perfect, or complete, or absolute in mathematical terms, meaning that nothing is left out. Again, take an incense bowl. Is there anything left out? We can say, "Well, it should have a top, the top is missing." At that moment we're pointing to something not there that we want to be there. We're coming out of our notions of what an incense bowl should look like.

There is a wonderful little story from the *Surangama Sutra* that illustrates the point I am making. Once upon a time there was a prince who, upon waking up, would look at himself in the mirror and exclaim, "Ah! Beautiful!" He was very handsome and he loved himself. One day he woke up and picked up the mirror the wrong way. Because the back of the mirror was not polished, he could not see his face in it and he panicked. "My head is gone! My head is gone! It's missing! It's missing!" He went completely berserk. Running into the streets yelling in this manner, he searched everywhere to find his missing head.

Eventually some friends saw him and grabbed him, saying, "You have your head. Why are you running around like this?" "No, my head is gone!" the prince insisted. They took him back to the palace but were unable to calm him down. They did not have straitjackets in those days, so they tied him to a pillar. He screamed so loudly they had to gag him. So there he was, bound and gagged, struggling to break loose so he could continue searching for his missing head. Finally, he got tired. (You can only struggle for so long.) When he had calmed down somewhat, one of his friends hit him in the face, and the prince shouted, "My head! It's there after all!"

For a few days he was beside himself with joy, telling everyone he'd found his head. His head was there, how wonderful! But when all his friends just looked at him in disbelief, he finally stopped being so exuberant about having found his head. It had always been there.

We have a notion that something is missing or not here, and one day we awaken to the fact that it *is* here, if only we could see it. And what is here? Just what we are, as we are. Our preconceptions and ideas block our acceptance and realization of this simple truth.

Because perfect means neither good nor bad, just what is as it is, even the murder of a child is perfect in this sense. It is just what it is. Good and bad are the judgments we add to what is—they're extra. Rain is what is. If we are farmers, we tend to say rain is wonderful; if we're planning a picnic, we think rain is terrible. But rain is rain. People say rain is wet, but a fish wouldn't. Water is the very essence of life to the fish, neither wet nor dry. The fish attaches no notions or dichotomies to it. When we say that something is perfect, we're pointing to this absence of dichotomy or dualism. Within the One Body, there is just one thing happening.

The brain functions in a dualistic way, breaking things up into this and that. It judges everything we do as good or bad, right or wrong. But good and bad, including the notion of evil, are extra. This does not mean that evil does not exist or that good and bad do not exist. It simply means that they're judgments that exist in the realm of the relative, colors we add to the thing itself. They're as the woof is to the warp, which brings me to the last word of the title, *Sutra.*

Sutra has several meanings. We have the English word *suture,* a joining or sewing of two together into one. Sutra also means warp, the threads that run through everything, the foundation threads of a weaving, or the interweaving of all things. The threads that run through everything *are* everything. So the sutra is the plane we hear flying outside. Breathing in and out is the sutra. All the discourses of this One Body are the sutra.

In weaving, the warp is the vertical threads, the woof the horizontal threads. For the warp, one chooses strings that are strong, unvariegated, simple, plain, without knots so they can tolerate lots of movement in any direction very easily. What the warp does is support the pattern and give it its basic tone. The threads of the woof don't have to be straight, usually they represent the pattern, so any threads can be used: splinters of wood, feathers, even horsehairs! The more complicated the weave, the more effect the color has on the tone. Together, the warp corresponds to the absolute, the woof to the relative; the weaving itself is their oneness. So the sutras are the strings or threads that run through everything, that allow all motion, all forms of life. But what is it that runs through everything and allows everything and anything to manifest?

Let's look at the word *Heart* in the title. As we have seen, the heart or essence of the Enlightened Way is not-knowing, which makes it possible for everything and anything to manifest. As soon as we know something, we prevent anything else from manifesting, from just popping up. As soon as we know something, we limit the thing we think we know. The state of not-knowing is everyone, everything, and anything, constantly manifesting, constantly popping up in accord with changes in time and situation. But if we live out of knowing, this endless manifestation of things, one after another, can't be experienced directly. We're blocked by our notions of what *should* be happening and get upset because our expectations don't match the way things really are. When we let go of our expectations, we are with things as they are, and we realize the essence or heart of the *Perfection of Great Wisdom Sutra*.

Maha Prajnaparamita Hrdaya Sutra: The whole message is

right here. If we could really see this word *maha,* see this One Body, see this one garden that is us, the world would look different. Instead of seeing trees, soil, manure, and flowers as different, separate things, we'd see them as One Body with different qualities, features, and characteristics. We'd see that when we cultivate the soil, we cultivate all the rest. Taking care of the tree affects the flowers; taking care of a flower affects the soil.

In the same way, we usually see the body as a limited, bound thing, yet we know that it has many features—hands, toes, numerous hairs and pores (all different), skin, bones, blood, guts, an assortment of organs, many feet of intestines. But they're all just one body with many, many features and characteristics. Hit one part and the whole feels it; the entire body is affected. Eat some food and what part is not affected? Breathe, what part is not affected?

Using the human body as a model of the One Body is a little misleading because the One Body has no outside or inside. We have to see this, we have to see maha. How do we see maha? We wake up!

2
Being-Doing

Avalokitesvara Bodhisattva, doing deep prajnaparamita,
Perceived the emptiness of all five conditions
And was freed of pain.

The word *Buddha* means Enlightened One, one who is awake.
Shakyamuni, an Indian prince who lived about 500 BCE, awakened after strenuous practice and was called Buddha. The substance of his enlightenment experience, the message he proclaimed, was: "How wonderful! How wonderful! Everything as it is is enlightened!" We, however, can't accept this fact because of our upside-down views that conceal this truth from us.

Shakyamuni Buddha's statement expresses two important aspects of our practice and life: the intrinsic and the experiential. Intrinsically, we are enlightened, we are the Buddha. Not just us, but everything—sticks, flowers, trees, stars. But experientially, we are not enlightened because we have yet to experience this fact. Without such experience, without such a realization, the intrinsic, though real, is just words to us.

Mahayana Buddhism makes an important distinction between someone who practices only to attain individual liber-

ation and the bodhisattva. The former feels that after realization there is nothing more to do. You get to the place where
you see what is, realize life as it is, and that's all there is to it.
The bodhisattva has also realized the true nature of life, but
has found that realization is not the end, that in fact it's the
beginning of practice. The bodhisattva has made a vow not to
remain in that state of oneness until every creature—human
and inhuman, animate and inanimate—has had the same realization. In effect, a bodhisattva (*bodhi* means "enlightenment"; *sattva* means "person") is one who does not stop at
individual realization or liberation.

Avalokitesvara Bodhisattva is the manifestation, or embodiment, of both prajna wisdom and compassion. Who is
this Avalokitesvara Bodhisattva? It is nothing other than us,
it is nothing other than who we intrinsically are. If we are really to see life, we must look at everything as ourselves. Instead, we say, "Okay, if I am supposed to be the embodiment
of prajna and compassion, how is it that I'm so deluded?
How come I cause so much suffering, so many problems?" In
so doing we separate ourselves from Avalokitesvara. We
must realize that Avalokitesvara is not separate—it's us! The
delusion is us, too! Everything is us.

. . . doing deep prajnaparamita

Some translations use the word *being* rather than *doing*. Being
deep prajnaparamita, one does deep prajnaparamita. Since
wisdom is the very state of what we are, being in that state
without separation is nothing but wisdom. Bodhisattvas, being
the state of enlightenment, do not remain or stop there, but in
order to help all of us, they purposely function, they do deep
prajnaparamita. This is compassion, which is the functioning
of wisdom. Because they are enlightened, they practice; be-

cause they're in the state of no-separation, which is wisdom, they practice compassion, the functioning of that state.

Perceived the emptiness . . .

Emptiness is a very important word in this sutra. In Sanskrit, it is *sunyata*; in Chinese Buddhism, it was translated as *ku*. One of the meanings of ku is "sky," which the Chinese used in order to convey the sense of the boundlessness that contains everything: the clouds, the planets, the stars. D. T. Suzuki's English translation of sunyata, emptiness, has many different connotations, one of which is "void," in the sense of there being nothing there. That's not what is meant here. Suzuki could just as well have used the word *fullness,* because sunyata is everything as it is, independent of all our notions. It's just this, directly perceived, without any ideas or concepts. Whatever notion we may have of emptiness is not emptiness, but merely an idea of emptiness.

If we look at a house, what we see is our concept of it. We look and say, "Oh yeah, that's a house." But what is a house? If we get a little closer, we might say there are walls and a roof. But if we take away the roof, do we still call it a house? If we take away the walls, do we still call it a house? If we leave only one wall up, we would no longer say it's a house, we'd probably say it's a wall. But what is a wall? If you start taking apart the wall, you have lumber. Where is the wall? We could look closely at the lumber. What is it? We could get down to the level of molecules. What is a molecule? Penetrating even more closely, we see the atoms. What is an atom? Then we get down to the so-called building blocks of the atom. What are they? Then down to energy. What is it?

One way of looking at emptiness is to see that everything is a notion, made up of other notions. When we tear apart the notions, nothing is left. But we can also look at emptiness without tearing anything apart. Just see everything as it is instead of the concept we have of it. The concept is not the thing itself. If we can get rid of all our ideas and concepts, what's left? This world as it is, and that's what emptiness means.

. . . of all five conditions

The five conditions are based on a traditional Buddhist classification of all things according to five fundamental elements of what we are (in Sanskrit, *skandhas*). My parents gave me the name Bernie many years ago. Later on, my teacher gave me the name Tetsugen. According to Buddhism, there is no such person as Bernie or Tetsugen, both are illusions. All of us have illusions about who we are and what the world is. According to Buddhist tradition, there are only five constituents, or skandhas, which are constantly changing and to which we give different names at different times.

My Dharma name, Tetsugen, consists of two words. *Gen* is a character that refers to the mysteries of life, but actually it is much more subtle than that. The connotation of gen is all those things that are right in front of you—so much in front of you, in fact, that you cannot see them. They're too intimate, too close. For example, as long as my stomach is healthy I'm not even aware it's there, it's such an intimate part of my body. When do I know it's there? When something goes wrong. Then I say, "I have a stomach ache," and suddenly I'm aware of my stomach—not the thing itself, but my concept of it. The same is true of Bernie. Much of the time I'm not even aware of Bernie. If I say, "Bernie is here," that is a delusion. In the same way that I am aware of my stomach only when there is something wrong with it, so I am only aware of Bernie when I set my thinking apart from myself.

Now let's look at the five elements or constituents. The first, form, refers both to internal biological functioning and to external physical appearances, which are always changing. The second comprises our feelings and sensations; the third, our perceptions and thoughts. The fourth refers to volition, impulse and reaction. It is associated with karma, our propensity to work, to do things in certain ways, which in turn is related to ethics and morality. The fifth is consciousness and comprises the entire psychological realm.

What Avalokitesvara saw is that these skandhas are all empty. Not just that Bernie is empty or that Bernie is just a notion of who I am, but that *all* these elements are nothing but notions or concepts that we make up and are thus devoid of independent reality.

. . . and was freed of pain.

This important line is not found in the original Sanskrit text but was added later in the Chinese translation. Being freed of pain does *not* mean there is no more pain! To realize that we are enlightened—and at the same time that everything as it is is enlightened—does not put a literal end to suffering or to what we call evil, nor does it put an end to problems in general. What is realized is that the suffering itself, the pain itself, is nothing but the functioning of the Enlightened Way. Having realized this, we take care of the suffering, we take care of the pain.

For example, I am enlightened and I gash my hand. Being enlightened does not mean that such a thing won't happen to me. My hand is gashed and blood spurts out—that is the functioning of the Enlightened Way. The fact that blood comes out when I cut my hand is prajna, wisdom. What do I immediately do? I take care of it. I do not stand around saying it is good or bad, evil or not evil; I just take care of it. Not being bound any longer by my notions of what it is, I deal with the reality directly. I don't avoid reality by standing around and letting my hand bleed. I deal with the thing itself—the bleeding gash—and not with notions about it such as whether it's good or bad, why did it happen to me, et cetera. I just take care of the gash. That's what is meant by being "freed of pain."

Many people practicing Zen think that after we practice zazen for a while, there will be no more problems. It's not that there are no more problems or pain, but that we know how to deal with them. We are intrinsically enlightened both before and after the experience of enlightenment. That means that whether we experience it or not, this is it. When we experience it—directly realize in our gut that this is it—things do not magically change somehow. This is *it*.

There was once a Jewish Messiah in the Middle East who had many, many followers. Now everybody knew that when the Messiah came, everything was supposed to be so-called nirvana, everything was supposed to be transformed in some miraculous way. So once his followers had accepted him as the Messiah, they were also obliged to accept the consequence—namely, that this was it. That although things did not seem to be what they were supposed to be, his coming meant that this was now paradise. *And yet everything was the same*!

Being told that we are prajnaparamita, that we are maha, that we are One Body, that we are enlightened, is meaningless unless we perceive it directly ourselves. We must experience this state of oneness, which is the state of reality itself. Having done so, we will be freed of pain in the midst of pain. We do not eliminate the pain; in fact, the point is not to eliminate anything. The realization that everything as it is is the Enlightened Way will not prevent someone from shooting a child. Nor will it demand that the enlightened person condone such an act. True realization, being beyond the realm of conceptualization, directly manifests in (and as) action. When my hand gets cut, I don't stand around saying, "Shall I do something about it or not?" I don't write books about it, nor do I ignore it. It cannot be ignored! Since both are part of this One Body, since the hand and I are not separate, when the hand gets cut, I take care of it. I do something.

The same is true with everything in life. I do something—not everything, which is impossible, but definitely something. Doing deep prajnaparamita means getting into the realm of what is, because in that state we are the One Body and have no choice. Our being and doing are no longer separate (as they are when we depend on conceptualization), they are just being-doing. This is doing deep prajnaparamita.

Let's return to the skandhas. Everything is an aggregate of these five conditions, which are all empty. There are also so-called passions associated with the five conditions. Associated with form is ignorance in the sense of darkness. We simply don't see what life is. The Chinese word for enlightenment actually consists of the ideograms for moon and sun put together. In other words, enlightenment is the brightest brightness there is. Ignorance is the negation of that, or no light at all.

Associated with sensation is pride, which arises out of ignorance. Associated with perception is desire. So out of our ignorance comes pride and out of our pride, desire, as in "I want this and do not want that." Though there is nothing intrinsically wrong with choosing, we should not be trapped by our desires. The passion associated with reaction is jealousy, which derives from desire: A person has what I desire so I become jealous. Conversely, I have pain that I wish to be rid of and, seeing someone without that pain, I become jealous. Finally, associated with consciousness is anger. Out of jealousy comes anger.

Suppose my two hands thought of themselves as separate entities with independent identities and consciousnesses. This hand is Joe, and that hand is Sam. If someone comes over to me with money, Sam reaches out for it and Joe gets jealous. First, Joe is ignorant of the fact that this is one body. He has pride in the fact that he is Joe, whereas the other is only Sam. Joe desires the money but Sam gets it, so out of that desire comes jealousy, and out of the jealousy comes anger, until Joe finally attacks Sam. One hand attacks the other! This goes on and on and on in the history of the world.

Let's look specifically at jealousy. There are so many wonderful people in the world. Shariputra was a disciple of Shakyamuni Buddha, who had ten or twelve major disciples, each of whom specialized in a different area. Shariputra was a specialist in wisdom, somebody else in compassion, somebody else in occult powers. Imagine if they had all been jealous of each other! We are all who we are; that's why this is a beautiful world.

If we are jealous of someone else, we are not appreciating ourselves enough. To drop the limited notion of self means to see the total self. Then we will really appreciate what we are doing and will do more to support those who are doing wonderful things. But as long as the self—the small self—intrudes, we become jealous. Then we only operate in the realm of the passions, the realm of the ego. But we also have to operate in this realm because we never eliminate these feelings, we simply transform them. For example, when the notion of self is transformed into an understanding of the One Body, jealousy becomes an act of support and love.

Also involved in the fifth condition, consciousness, is our capacity to decide on an action independent of our inclination. Free will and determinism enter here. From the perspective of the fourth condition (reaction, karma, volition, and impulse), everything seems determined. We have certain reactions and that is the end of it. But the fifth condition says that at any instant our action is not determined, but is open, complete, and free. One does not really negate the other, though logically this seems to be the case.

I should say more about enlightened functioning. We have many notions about what this functioning is supposed to be. One notion has to do with the so-called nonattachment of the enlightened person. If my child is in tremendous pain and suffering, being enlightened, I *become* that tremendous pain and suffering. In other words, not only am I affected by it, I am tremendously affected by it because there is no separation between my child and me. Before realization, I would ask questions such as "How can I stop this?" or "Why is this happening to my child?" After realization, I simply do the best I can to take care of things. I don't just accept them, I take care of them.

If I am driving down the road and see a dead dog, I might think, "Thank God that's not me." The dead dog brings up thoughts of death, I become full of pain and sorrow. That is nonacceptance of what is happening. Thinking I am separate, I may do a variety of things—I may run away, I may stop and bury the dog—but a lot of ideas enter my mind and prevent a direct response. Once I realize this is all One Body, however, I feel that in this dead dog a part of me has died, so I get out and take care of it. Not clinging to the notion of death, I act. True nonattachment is to be neither separate from nor clinging to what is. Instead of living in the realm of ideas and feelings about whatever is happening, we live in the realm of action.

We're like a mirror. Whatever comes before the mirror is there; when it leaves, it's simply gone. Rather than littering each changing moment with the things that have happened or are going to happen or may happen, we deal with what is.

There's a story in the *Dhammapada* about someone who was

shot by an arrow. A person comes to pull it out, but even as the arrow is threatening to end his life, the fellow says, "Before you do that, can you tell me what type of feathers were used on that arrow? If I know that, I'll know which tribe shot the arrow." Or, "Can you tell me what type of wood the arrow is made of?" The Buddha says that such a person is obviously going to die because of his attachment to these questions. The thing to do, of course, is to pull out the arrow!

All of us tend to suffer in this way, asking endless questions instead of acting. Freed of pain does not mean that we avoid pain and suffering, it means we pull out the arrow.

There is an interesting saying about a horse: It's best to ride a horse in the direction it's going. There is not much choice. This means total acceptance of what is, yet without the implication that we don't act. Total acceptance is not at all passive. Accept this situation because this is it—and change it. We have to change it. We don't have the choice of not changing it, because life is change. We must accept that, too. There is no way that any situation can stay as it is. Change is nothing but the very functioning of life itself.

We all have a time bomb inside us; we *are* this time bomb. I am going to die the very next instant, so I am doing the best I can this instant. I think all of us must function in the best way we can. To say that everything is changing is to say that everything is going to die this very instant. So we must do the very best we can each moment, as if each moment were our last— because it is!

3
Emptiness

Shariputra, form is no other than emptiness, emptiness no other
than form;
Form is precisely emptiness, emptiness precisely form.

As I said in Chapter 2, Shariputra was a disciple of Shakyamuni Buddha and renowned for his understanding of prajna
wisdom. Shakyamuni had many wonderful disciples. His
sangha was very large, like a beautiful garden. On the one
hand, a garden is just this One Body, one sangha, one community, one life; and on the other hand, it's all the myriad
lives and beings in the garden, completely interdependent
and, at the same time, completely unique. This mutual interdependence means that each one of us is totally affected by
every other thing in the garden. Another way of expressing
this is to say that the part is the whole and the whole is the
part.

Since Zen is this One Body, life itself, it excludes nothing.
Many people think that Zen excludes things like ritual or reli-
gion or science. If you say that, you don't understand what Zen
is because you don't understand what life is. Zen is life. Zen is
this—this moment, this stick, this thisness. Take anything

away from this, and it's no longer this. Such a truth should be obvious, but we have to practice to realize it.

The major disciples of Shakyamuni Buddha, each unique and with different attributes, together became the strength of the sangha. Hundreds of thousands of students of the Way were affected and trained by these major disciples. Each of us *is* each of these major disciples. I am wisdom, I am understanding, I am compassion, and so forth. I also am myself, with my own unique gifts. But when we don't perceive this One Body and our interdependence, jealousy, and competition arise.

Form is no other than emptiness, emptiness no other than form;

Two different statements are being made in this one sentence. Form is dharma, phenomena, the phenomenal world; it stands for manyness, the differences of life, all the forms that we see. Emptiness refers to the oneness of life, which means life as it is, without any distinctions. The sutra is saying that form, or all things, is no other than emptiness, no other than the One Body.

I was trained as a mathematician, and in mathematics one of the things we search for is called an isomorphism, a relationship of sameness between two apparently different classes of objects. An isomorphic relationship implies that two different worlds, or worlds that seem very different, are really the same. Similarly, "Form is no other than emptiness, emptiness no other than form" implies that form and emptiness are isomorphically related. Although we look at the world of phenomena as being very different from the world of oneness, in fact the two are not different at all.

This means that if we can really see the world of oneness, then we understand everything. Isn't this amazing? The other way is so long. To try to understand everything without going through the world of emptiness is simpler as far as each detail is concerned, but it takes time—forever, in fact! This way is so much shorter: Just understand one thing, emptiness, and you understand everything.

In Zen study, we are concerned with three things: the world of differences (form), the world of emptiness (oneness), and the relationship between the two (which is called harmony). This is also how we study the Three Treasures: the Buddha, which refers to the world of oneness; the Dharma, which is the world of form; and the Sangha, or the relationship that says the two are really the same thing. We begin such study the simple way, by seeing the world of oneness, of emptiness.

What is emptiness? That is, what is anything when we take away all our notions and ideas? What is a stick when I take away all my notions of what it is? We say, "a stick." Take that idea away. "Straight." Take that away. "An extension of my hand." Take that away. What is it? Once we see what it is, then we see everything. This is the first part of Zen study.

The second part is seeing the differences, having seen the emptiness of all things. Having seen this as it is, now appreciate it as a stick, as straight, as an extension of my hand, as not you, as not me, as not the room. In the first part of Zen study, the stick is all those things. In fact, it's everything, because one sees that it's all one thing, One Body. Now appreciate it as *not* being this incense bowl, *not* being this stand, and so on. This one thing *is* the myriad things and the myriad not-things. That's form.

Again, in the first part of our study, we see how all things are no other than emptiness, no other than this One Body. God, flowers, trees, manure, insects, worms, and butterflies are One Body. Having seen it as One Body, we then see it as all the differences, which is the second part of the study. In the third part, we see the relationship—both are the same.

When we see that form is empty and that diversity is oneness, when we truly see what that means, we achieve prajna. But please remember that whether we see this or not, we are intrinsically prajna. We are everything, but we have to realize it, we have to experience it. When we do, that is nirvana so far as Zen study is concerned. Realizing prajna is leaving the world of attachments, the world of samsara. Once we realize there is no fixed form, we are no longer attached to the world of form. Similarly, when we clearly see that emptiness is form, that oneness is all forms, we achieve compassion. For everything in life is that oneness, everything in life is me. Compassion implies that we're no longer attached to dwelling in the world of nirvana. Then we can appreciate the statement that nirvana is samsara, enlightenment is delusion. Similarly, seeing that form is emptiness, we see that samsara is nirvana, and delusion is enlightenment.

Form is precisely emptiness, emptiness precisely form.

Emptiness is. Form is. In the analogy of the house, we discovered that one way to find emptiness is by using a kind of reductive analysis culminating with the finding that there is nothing there at all. That is, we can take a stick and put it under a microscope. As we go deeper and deeper, we find more and more space and less and less substance. It's not long before what we are seeing does not look like a stick at all. All we see is wood. When we blow that up, we don't even see the wood anymore, we see the so-called molecular structure. If we keep increasing the magnification, all of a sudden, all we see is space. There is nothing there!

But we don't have to do all that to find emptiness. Our stick is precisely emptiness as it is. When we see emptiness, it is precisely form; that is, emptiness should not be understood in a nihilistic way, as if there is nothing there. Emptiness is just everything as it is.

"Form is precisely emptiness, emptiness precisely form" is, in a way, the key line of the sutra. It's the beginning of the explanation of prajna wisdom, the functioning of the state of emptiness. Emptiness in itself is a very passive thing, it's just as it is. The functioning of emptiness, however, is very active.

We have two terms that we use in this regard: Great Death and Great Rebirth. Great Death is seeing that everything is just one thing, that there are no separate entities. There is no me; I have completely died. Everything has died the Great Death. There are no sticks, no flowers, no trees. When we truly see that state, that moment is also the Great Rebirth, which is seeing that everything exists and functions beautifully and totally as is. They are the same state. Just as one cannot have Great Death without Great Rebirth, so one cannot have prajna wisdom without compassion (or vice versa). Compassion is just the functioning of prajna wisdom. It's like a candle: You light it and there is a flame. Sometimes we say the flame is prajna wisdom and the light, which is the functioning of the flame, is compassion. They are completely inseparable.

In practice, we tend to stick to just one side of reality—the absolute rather than the relative, prajna rather than compassion, emptiness rather than phenomena. Much of Zen practice is about learning to see both sides so clearly that they both disappear, at which point we can move freely from one side to the other or talk about either side without getting stuck in one-sided views. The two sides are not different; they are the same world. What world is it? *This* world, this very moment! If we see just this, we see all there is to see in Buddhism and all there is to see in life. Buddhism, after all, is just an expression for the Enlightened Way, which is what life is. To realize the Enlightened Way is nothing other than realizing this very moment.

Wisdom and compassion, in effect, are two different descriptions of the oneness of this moment. Let's look a little further at compassion. When you see that emptiness, or the state of oneness, includes all forms just as they are, you see that the functioning of emptiness means loving God, loving my spouse, loving my student, loving my children, loving my neighbor, loving myself. The state of compassion implies liberation from attachment to emptiness. Some people tend to get stuck in that state of oneness, of "form is emptiness," of just being without doing, which is a very passive state. By contrast, compassion is the extremely active functioning of that state of oneness.

The love spoken of in Christianity seems to me the same as Buddhist compassion, because like compassion, Christian love derives from and is the functioning of the state of poverty. My notion of poverty is nonattachment, which is the state of prajna or no-separation. Being in that state, whatever we do is a compassionate act, because compassion is simply the functioning of that state of oneness. Remember my gashed hand? Being one with it, I take care of it; that's a compassionate act. However, if I am separate from it, even though I take care of it, that's not a compassionate act. These acts may look the same, but in fact they are not.

Another example: A child in the street is about to be hit by a truck. I see the truck coming down the street and without thinking, just being totally one with what's happening, I run out and push the child out of the way. After the truck has gone by I may get up and yell at the child, but this too is compassionate because it's coming from the state of oneness, because it's the functioning of this prajna.

Now let's say the same thing happens, and this time I'm not operating from the place of oneness. I may think, "The child is going to be hurt! But that truck might hit me." Although I still run and save the child, then get up and yell at him, in this case

I am yelling because I almost got hurt. That's not the functioning of prajna because separation exists. No prajna, no compassion. If you are one with the situation, you function, and that functioning is compassion. If you're not, that functioning is not compassion.

(At the same time, because everything as it is is prajna, including my worrying about getting hurt, everything is also the functioning of prajna, including my yelling at the child out of my own self-concern. So how are these two cases different? I leave this for you to ponder by yourself.)

Let's go back to the parable of a man pierced by an arrow. With the arrow piercing me, I'm not separate from the situation, and having no doubts, I pull it out. But then I stop and say, "Did I do that the right way?" At that moment separation has occurred. When I pulled out the arrow, the act was spontaneous: no opinion, no right or wrong, no discrimination. Similarly, when it's raining and I get wet, it's just raining and I just get wet, whether or not I think this is good or bad.

Let's say I am talking with a friend, telling him I don't like the way he's living his life. He's not eating well and I want to give him some money. Is that right or wrong? If my doing this is free from any notion of what I am giving him, if it's just a total act expressing the oneness of life, the question of right and wrong is beside the point. All that happens is just giving. However, if I give him money because I don't like the way he is living so I want to help him out, there is separation. That separation, the dualism, is what's wrong. Whether we think the act itself is right or wrong is beside the point. So long as that separation is there, because notions of self and other are there, the action is dualistic. It violates the integrity of the One Body.

The doubt about whether what you are doing is right or wrong takes place in the world of forms, of the relative, of dualism. This does not imply that this world is invalid; on the contrary, it is the same world as the world of oneness. Can you see that? One does not negate the other. The world of dualism and dichotomy is not a bad world. It is actually isomorphic with the world of oneness, which some people mistakenly perceive as the only good world. Although these worlds are distinct (not-one), they are nonetheless the same (not-two).

Another sort of doubt pertains to the world of oneness. Although we are actually functioning in both worlds at the same time (they are the same world), most of us don't perceive the world of oneness. We have no notion—or only a notion—of what oneness really means. Because we haven't actually experienced this oneness, the word does not speak to our guts, only to our head. And so long as this is so, our functioning will not change or even shift. The way to see this oneness and remove all doubt is by simply letting go of the self, because it's the self that prevents us from seeing it. The self is our heavy baggage of concepts and ideas.

Once we fully realize the Enlightened Way, we no longer have any doubts or questions about the true nature of reality and existence; all that's left is the functioning of that realization. At this point, it may be useful to distinguish between different degrees of realization experiences. When we speak of realization, we usually mean seeing our true nature, the enlightenment experience. When this seeing is truly profound, we speak of great enlightenment, after which the last doubts disappear.

Until we get to the place—and we will—where there is no more doubt, we must clear away that doubt through practice. And practice does not stop when there is no more doubt. From the top of the mountain we have to climb down. Practice never stops. To better understand the endless character of practice-realization, let's imagine a pitch-black room in which we're at first unable to see anything at all. Then something happens and a little light appears. Now we see what the room looks like, but not really. It's still not very clear and we are not satisfied or happy with our perception of the room, so we add more and more light. Even when there is quite a lot of light, we are still unable to see the room in total clarity, but at least we feel confident that this is the room. We know what's there and how to function in it. But in order to really take care of things, we must vacuum and dust every day, and for all this much light is needed.

There are many different ways, many different paths. What is important is whether we really practice or whether we just play around. Really practicing means letting go of the self. But usually what we want is to gain something rather than let go, so we go searching (like the prince in the story) for something extra, some new head to put on top of our own. Instead, we have to stop, sit still, and just let go. This is not simple except for a very few. But what if it takes a thousand eons? If we practice and let go, it's worth it! Don't worry about time, just do it. Don't worry about when realization will come, just do the practice. Just do deep prajnaparamita, and the rest will take care of itself.

Here is a story that illustrates what I mean by really practicing. Once, in the days of Shakyamuni Buddha, there was a retarded monk who wanted very much to be enlightened. Although he was unable to read or do any of the things the other monks did, he had faith in Shakyamuni. So Shakyamuni said, "You want to be enlightened? Well, there is a way. First, sit in that corner of the room." The monk agreed and sat in that corner. Then Shakyamuni threw a ball at him and it hit him. Shakyamuni said, "Okay, now bring me the ball and go sit in that corner." Again the monk agreed, and again Shakyamuni hit him with the ball. After Shakyamuni had done this in all four corners of the room, he said, "Now sit in the middle of the room, and you will be enlightened." Because of his faith, the monk sat in the middle of the room and he became enlightened!

Although there are many ways to practice and each is different, practice always boils down to the same thing: We must let go completely, as completely as this retarded monk. Usually we practice in order to acquire or gain something, not to let go. We start sitting because we want to become better in some way—to improve our physical well-being, become more intelligent or more stable, experience samadhi or even enlightenment—the list is endless. Usually practice is a matter of what we want to gain. But the message that keeps coming back (from the practice itself, as it were) is: "Let go! Let go! Let go!" To which we usually respond, "I don't want to. I want to be taught." But again what the practice keeps saying is, "Let go!"

4

Letting Go

Sensation, perception, reaction, and consciousness are also
* like this.*
O Shariputra, all things are expressions of emptiness:
Not born, not destroyed; not stained, not pure; neither waxing
* nor waning.*
Thus emptiness is not form,
Not sensation nor perception, reaction nor consciousness;
No eye, ear, nose, tongue, body, mind;
No color, sound, smell, taste, touch, thing;
No realm of sight, no realm of consciousness;
No ignorance, no end to ignorance;
No old age and death, no cessation of old age and death;

When the *Heart Sutra* says that form is emptiness, it's
speaking not just of the first skandha (or condition), but of
all five. All five conditions are empty, so the sutra says that
all five conditions "are also like this." That is, whatever
comes up—not just physical form, but all the various func-
tionings of the mind—is empty; and emptiness in turn is all
of these forms.

O Shariputra, all things are expressions of emptiness:

Instead of things, which we associate with fixed substances, it might be useful here to speak of phenomena, for which the Buddhist term is *dharmas,* which are insubstantial, momentary events. At any rate, dharmas and phenomena are approximately equivalent. All phenomena—anger, love, animals, ghosts, humans, demons, minerals, grass, laughter, unicorns—are manifestations of emptiness. That's what emptiness is: the vegetables growing in the soil; the vegetables we are eating, have eaten, and will eat; laughter, joy, anger, sorrow, pain, suffering, and misery; you and me. All of these without exception are nothing but expressions of emptiness.

So what is emptiness? All of these phenomena *without* the labels associated with them. For example, laughter is an expression of emptiness. But what is it independent of, or apart from, the word *laughter,* the notion of laughter? Pain is pain, but what is it when removed from the notion of pain? If you take away all the labels, the ideas about things, *that* is emptiness. Talking, rubbing my nose, the microphone, the speakers, our breathing, the flowers, children starving, dogs being run over by cars—all are expressions of emptiness.

Not born, not destroyed; not stained, not pure; neither waxing nor waning.

The first quality of all phenomena is that they're empty. The second is that everything is impermanent. All that exists is change. There is no such thing as permanence; all phenomena are not born, not destroyed.

One of our delusions is to think that everything is permanent. Another is to think that everything is impermanent. Both are delusions! "Not born, not destroyed" means timeless.

And at the same time, everything is impermanent. At every instant, everything is completely new.

If you look at the species of oak called live oak, from one point of view the oak appears ageless, as if it would never die. But if you look closely, there are leaves dropping, buds forming, and new leaves growing. It's always dying at this very moment. It's simultaneously death and birth, and at the same time there is no death and no birth. The tree is just a tree.

At every moment everything is completely changing. *This* is all there is—just movement, just change. In this moment there is no such concept as change, as past, present, or future. The notion of change implies that there is a future or a past. When we say that all is change we don't mean this notion of change, we mean that everything is right here, right now. This is it. For example, Shakyamuni Buddha did not live around 500 BCE and Christ did not live five centuries later. No, they're right here now! You think you can read a history book and find out about Shakyamuni Buddha? No, he is right here, right now. How do you change the life of Shakyamuni Buddha? *You* change and *he* is changed. Everything is right here, right now. Thus, everything we do affects all past, present, and future, because it's all right here, right now—not born, not destroyed.

The fifth skandha or condition, if you recall, is consciousness. Actually, we talk about eight types of consciousness, including those associated with the six senses (ear, eye, nose, tongue, touch, and mind). In addition, there is a consciousness related to the notion of ego and another we call the *alaya* or "storehouse" consciousness. One of my teachers, Koryu Osaka Roshi, once mentioned that the alaya consciousness contained everything: all past, present, and future. That seemed a little strange to me at the time. I could see my actions affecting the present and the future, but how could they affect the past?

And I could see the storehouse consciousness containing the past and present, but how could it contain the future? But Koryu Roshi said, "Yes, it contains everything. Why? Because it is *now*! There is no past, there is no future. There is not even a present!"

In our linear way of thinking we are able to see that if we change something now, that changes the future. But we have a hard time seeing that if we change something now, the past is changed as well. Yet this is true because past, present, and future are nothing but notions. It's all right now. In fact, one obvious sense of how we change the past is that the past exists only as we see it. If we see it differently, the past is all changed—immediately.

The first of the Buddha's Four Noble Truths is that life is suffering. We suffer for many reasons: because we don't have what we want; because we have what we want; because we have what we don't want; because we have what we want but it's fading away; because we're fading away and getting old; because we're not old enough. But apart from all these so-called reasons, the question is: What is it? Why do we suffer? We suffer because we can't be satisfied with what we have or with what is—even though, of course, we don't really have anything. We suffer because the grass is green and we want it to be purple. We suffer because we don't see and accept things as they are.

There are two delusions concerning suffering. One is that everything is suffering, and the other is that there is no suffering, that everything is okay. The point here is that *any* idea we have is a delusion. Can we accept that? Can we accept that things as they are—"not stained, not pure"—are reality and that our concepts of them are delusions? We are responsible for the concepts of pure and impure, good and bad. We add on the notions of being born and dying; strictly speaking, they too are extraneous. When we see our lives independent of all these notions, we see directly that we don't die nor are we born, that we're timeless. We suppose that at some time something is born and at another time something dies. That's just our notion; birth and death are not inherent qualities of phenomena as they are.

Eventually we understand that there is no entity, self, or fixed substance. Physicists have been looking for the basic building block of all existence for a long time, but I don't believe they will ever find it. I don't believe there is a basic building block. As soon as you think you've found it, you discover that it too is empty. It's only another concept and you must go further.

All things are "neither waxing nor waning." No loss, no gain; spaceless space. There's nothing to add because there is nothing to begin with! There is no basic entity—just spaceless space, timeless time, all empty, all without qualities. So what's left? Just what is. It's so simple.

Thus emptiness is not form,
Not sensation nor perception, reaction nor consciousness;

Emptiness is not the five skandhas (conditions). In many translations, this line is translated as: "So *in* emptiness there is no form . . . [my italics]" *Chu,* the word translated as "in," is also often translated as "middle," as in the Middle Way. But the Middle Way does not mean something in the middle, a path between this and that. The Middle Way is the Way; it's equivalent to an equal sign (=). So it is not so much that *in* emptiness there is no form, but rather that emptiness is equal to no form. Emptiness is defined here as equivalent to not-form, not-sensation, not-perception, not-reaction, not-consciousness. In short, whatever your notion of it may be, that's not it. Drop all your notions and *that* is emptiness! So what is it? Just what is!

Not-form, not-sensation, not-perception, and so on do not mean there's no form, no sensation, no perception. They mean when we take away the notion of form, we have just form as it is; when we take away the notion of sensation, we have just sensation as it is, and so forth. Zen koans refer to talking without using our lips or tongues. That doesn't mean we're not talking; it means we're just talking. There's no separate notion of talking (or not-talking). Or take once more the example of the stomach. When our stomach is just functioning, there is, in a sense, no-stomach functioning. We only think of it as our stomach when it doesn't function well anymore, when it's sick or in pain. We only think about it when it's no longer just functioning, when we are no longer just functioning. So we may say that there is a stomach only when there is something wrong, only when there's separation, when we and the stomach are not just functioning. Similarly, the negation in the sutra, "no eye," signifies just seeing, which is not seeing with the eye but with the whole being.

No eye, ear, nose, tongue, body, mind;
No color, sound, smell, taste, touch, thing:
No realm of sight, no realm of consciousness.

We say there are eighteen elements: six sense organs (the mind is considered the sixth sense organ); the objects of these six sense organs; and the six corresponding worlds or realms associated with them. The sutra negates all of them.

We could consider all these things as things we have—eye, ear, nose, tongue, body, mind, et cetera. In general, we tend to define the self in terms of what we think we have. But in reality, we have nothing! In Hebrew, we don't say "I have," we say "yesh li," which means "there is to me." We say, "There is to me a pen," not "I have a pen." Or "There is to me intelligence," not "I have intelligence." That's how I look at life. There happens to be some money in my pocket at this point, but it's not mine. I don't have money. It happens to be there now, but it will be moving on tomorrow. I don't have anything. We are all traveling salesmen, all we have is the baggage we carry at this moment. We have no intrinsic qualities, no attributes or characteristics, not even intelligence. There is simply what is as it is (free from our notion of having). Just *this*!

Similarly, we don't have a self or fixed identity. This notion of permanence, this idea that there is some kind of entity called "I," is a distorted view. I think I am Bernie or Tetsugen. I am neither; those are only notions. Because everything is changing, what actually exists is nothing. We can think of this nothing as formless energy, and things like self, money, and beauty as manifestations of energy, insubstantial mirages to which we try vainly to give substance.

Because there is no I to begin with, it is wonderfully easy to give, for there is no one giving anything to anyone! Things just flow from one point to another ceaselessly. Those people who are unable to give are stuck; they block this universal formless energy. T'ai chi is a practice that allows the chi (energy) to flow freely. If you block the chi, what happens? You get sick. Block anything that seeks to happen, and you get sick. Holding on is as crazy as refusing to release the pressure from a pressure cooker—it will surely explode. Let it go. Things flow where they are supposed to flow because we don't own them. We hold on because we think we own them. Thinking in terms of owning, having, or being something just ties us up, we become the pressure cooker. Just let it go!

The same thing is true of our practice. Let go! But we refuse, we hold on to everything. We completely attach to our notions of how things are instead of seeing them as they really are; thus, we're unable to act freely in any situation. We create our own fetters. Those fetters are our ideas; we refuse to let go of them. In this way we bind and tie ourselves up more and more—in the name of our ideas, our feelings, even in the name of freedom!

In Buddhism, we speak of a twelvefold chain of *nidanas* (conditions) that serves to explain how our life is generated. The first link in this chain is ignorance, or lack of light. We don't see what is happening; consequently, our actions are determined by our karma, our propensity to do certain things in certain ways. With our sense organs, we see certain things or feel or hear them; therefore, we have sensations and feelings that seem pleasant, unpleasant, or neutral. Because of these feelings or sensations and our judgments about them ("This is pleasant" or "This is unpleasant"), we have desires, attachments, and cravings. As a result of these, we cling to the objects we desire. Then habitual patterns form and there is becoming. Because of that, in turn, things are born—new personalities, new situations; and because of that, decay and death occur. It is an endless cycle.

Shakyamuni Buddha taught that this chain of conditions could be broken at any point. The way we break it is to let go of the self. That's all—let go of the self! It's not so much that the chain is broken, it's transformed. Just as earlier we spoke about the passions being transformed, here, if we let go of the self, the whole pattern of conditions is transformed.

No ignorance, no end to ignorance;
No old age and death, no cessation of old age and death;

Here the twelve conditions are being negated and the negation is itself negated. In addition, what I just said about breaking the chain by eliminating the self and transforming it, is being negated, too. There is no ignorance and no end to ignorance. These twelve conditions that we study in Buddhist philosophy are empty. They're nothing but notions. In fact, *everything* we study is another notion about life, not life itself.

Ignorance is the first link in the chain of conditions, and death is the last. The sutra goes through the whole list and, item after item, negates every basic tenet of Buddhism—and it negates the negation too. It points directly to this moment. All of these concepts and notions are what we are constantly adding to this moment.

No eye, ear, nose, tongue, body, mind;
No color, sound, smell, taste, touch, thing;
No realm of sight, no realm of consciousness;
No ignorance, no end to ignorance;
No old age and death, no cessation of old age and death;

Referring to this section of the sutra, Koryu Osaka Roshi once said, "Nothing in those five lines exist, and even the five lines themselves do not exist!" If we can negate all of it, we have the Great Death and the Great Rebirth. In the *Heart Sutra*, negation is affirmation.

If you read metaphysics (for example, Aristotle's principle of self-identity or noncontradiction), you learn that if you deny self-identity (that A equals A), you wind up with the absurd consequence that all things become one. If you say that A equals A and also that A does not equal A, you derive a basic contradiction, which can't be allowed because it leads to the result that all things are one. (An infinite number of statements follow from a contradiction.) This wonderful absurdity is what Buddhism considers reality! Since A does not equal A (since there is no fixed self), A is the whole universe!

How can we relate the One Body to relationships? Being related is not a matter of going around saying, "We are One Body!" We let go of that, we just *are* One Body. Being One Body, the relationship is complete and perfect as is, and the needs of each part are taken care of. Whenever anything happens that requires a response, I respond, I take care of what has to be done. This is compassion as the functioning of prajna. Similarly, in relationships, when we both really see that we are One Body, we get to the point where we no longer think about it—we just are. Take the example of the baby and the mother. For a certain period they are literally one body. When the child cries or needs something, it is automatically taken care of by the mother without any separation into baby and mother. This is true prajna. It's also pure love. Shakyamuni Buddha used the same analogy; he said, "Everything is my child." Now just imagine we really functioned as if everything were our child, as if we were not separate from anything.

This is One Body, whether we talk about a spouse, a garbage collector, or a child. The One Body is just whatever is happening and our immediate response to whatever is happening. If the child is hungry, we feed him; if he has a cut, we take care of him. Or say there are twins and both are crying. You are the parent. What do you do? It depends on the situation. Here is this one body and both hands get cut. What do you do? There are no guidelines. Being one body, you just do what's necessary. This one looks worse for some reason, so you take care of it first. The point is you function *directly* because this is one body. It's not a matter of composing some set of guidelines for decision making. The realization of One Body enables us to function directly, immediately, and appropriately. Appropriateness is not something judged or decided by somebody else; appropriateness means that we deal with things as best we can.

Please note that nowhere here is there any notion of an end

to suffering. Those two children are crying and you can only deal with one at a time. That means the other one will suffer. Realizing the One Body simply means that you no longer sit around trying to figure out how to deal with the problem. You act; you do something! There are no utopias. When we are enlightened, we accept samsara as it is and function directly in samsara. This is nirvana. There is no nirvana other than this.

Reality is nothing but what is happening right here, right now. Things just happen, just move, just change. We can't pin them down by taking a snapshot. That's what all our ideas and concepts amount to—a pile of snapshots. We just have to see *this* directly. That's the state of emptiness, while the snapshots constitute the world of form. And the *Heart Sutra* is saying, once again, that these two worlds are the same.

5

No Suffering

No suffering, no cause or end to suffering, no path . . .

This line refers to the Four Noble Truths expounded by Shakyamuni Buddha in his first teaching. He said that life—all existence, everything—is nothing but *dhukka*, which is commonly translated as "suffering." This is the First Noble Truth. The Second Noble Truth declares that there is a cause of suffering, and that is the fact that everything is change, or movement. What we seek is permanence. We want there to be an ego, an atom, something solid that we can grab on to, some tangible, ultimate truth. Since this is the case, we are bound to suffer, to constantly bang into the fact that things don't go the way we want. Things go the way things go.

For example, we think we're human beings, but Buddhism recognizes six realms of existence (or psychological states), only one of which is human, and we continuously transmigrate through these realms or states, moment after moment. We think of ourselves as exclusively human; Buddhism says that sometimes we are human, sometimes we are demons, and sometimes we're hungry ghosts. A hungry ghost has a needle-thin neck and a huge belly. Because there is no way for food to enter, the hungry ghost is constantly hungry, thirsty, and unsatisfied. In the human realm, conceptual processing of moment-after-moment change takes place; hence, it is the realm characterized by delusion.

We are constantly transmigrating and because this is all One Body, so is everything else. Sometimes we are like fighting warriors; sometimes we are in heaven. For example, someone may come to me and say that her sitting is pure bliss. But this is not such a wonderful state because it's lost almost immediately. On the other hand, someone who is in hell comes to me, his body shaking with torment. Although there's tremendous pain and agony, it has to get better because it's impossible for us to remain in any of these realms or states. We can't even stay in the human realm, far less in heaven or hell.

Nevertheless, there is an end to suffering—that's the Third Noble Truth. Isn't this wonderful? Shakyamuni not only said that all is suffering, he not only discovered the cause of suffering, he also said there's a solution. One way to put an end to suffering is to live life as it is, which we do by eliminating misconceptions. Since any conception is a misconception, we let go of our attachment to our concepts and ideas, to our notions of self, permanence, ego, atom, or whatever. With these attachments out of the way—when we don't know—we experience life as it is.

This is readily tested in the laboratory of life by paying attention to how much we keep banging into things, such as expectations. When we no longer do this, we no longer suffer. When we speak of putting an end to suffering, this does not mean that suffering and pain are at an end, but rather that, being one with pain, there is no separation. There is no subject who suffers and no object that is suffered. In this sense the suffering is gone.

Egocentric suffering, which is fundamentally neurotic,

should be distinguished from selfless suffering. Because of our attachment to the notion of self, we have egocentric suffering, which tends to make us inactive, to withdraw into ourselves, to contract in a kind of death. When we let go of the self, we have selfless suffering, which is still suffering—because life is suffering—but is active, expansive, and dynamic. It is not deathlike, but alive with growth and expansion. Sensing directly the suffering of the world, we expand to take care of it.

Whenever the self is present, we contract; when the self is absent, we expand. Take the example of the man shot by an arrow. In the case of egocentric suffering, the man's response is to freeze up: "Why did this happen to me? What am I going to do? I have this arrow sticking in me!" Egocentric suffering does not enter the world of immediate action; it exists in the world of notions and concepts. But in the case of selfless suffering, the man simply removes the arrow. One response is life-denying and the other is life-affirming. Selfless suffering is the functioning of prajna wisdom, and this is what we call compassion.

The Fourth Noble Truth is that the way to end suffering is the Eightfold Path. The first aspect of this path is right view or right understanding; second, right thought; third, right words or right speech; fourth, right conduct or karma; fifth, right livelihood; sixth, right effort; seventh, right mindfulness; and eighth, right concentration or samadhi. The word *right*, which precedes all these aspects, is not used in the usual dualistic sense of right as opposed to wrong. In this context right means "non-," as in nonconcept or nonview. Eliminate all concepts and you have right view. Then go one step further and eliminate nonview as well.

What do "right words or right speech" mean? Shakyamuni Buddha taught constantly for fifty years, from the time of his enlightenment until his death. He was always surrounded by students and disciples and constantly preaching the Dharma. But when he was about to die, he said that for those fifty years he had not said a single word! That's right speech. Too many of us think we know what is right and go around telling others how things should be. This is not right speech. Speaking without speaking, without lips or tongue, speaking spontaneously without the filters constructed by the mind, speaking with the whole being, just speaking—that's right speech.

Similarly, right effort means noneffort. If I separate myself from what I am doing, or if I see myself as doing anything at all, it's not right effort. Totally doing what has to be done without separation from the deed is noneffort—nothing is being done!

Again this "non-" seems like ordinary negation, but it actually implies radical affirmation; what it negates is all our notions and ideas, not the action. When I let go of all my ideas about an action, I'm not separate from either action or nonaction, which is right action. Similarly, right samadhi does not mean good samadhi, as when students come in and tell me, "Wow! That sitting was really great. I was in tremendous samadhi!" When one knows that one is in great samadhi, one is not in samadhi at all. When there's samadhi, it's nonsamadhi in the sense that we are completely unaware of it. Being aware of our samadhi means that we are in a sort of dream world constructed of notions of good and bad samadhi. Instead of entertaining such notions, just sit. Become sitting. This just sitting or nonsitting, or nonsamadhi is samadhi!

The Eightfold Path sets forth eight different ways of letting go. Over and over it emphasizes letting go and just totally being this moment. In a way, it's crazy to speak about totally being this moment because intrinsically there is no way not to totally be this moment; this moment is what we are, this is our true nature. But experientially we must speak this way. We have to realize that totally being this moment is what we actually are. Merely knowing this in an intellectual way does us no good at all.

In "No suffering, no cause or end to suffering; No path . . . ," the *Heart Sutra* negates the Four Noble Truths, but once again, this negation is really affirmation. Life is radically affirmed by negating any notion we have of it. If you say all life is suffering, that's just another idea, another concept. Life is not suffering—*this* is life, this very moment as it is, independent of all notions. Whatever words or ideas we want to add to it are not life; they are our way of talking about life, our snapshots and descriptions of it.

The implication of "No suffering, no cause or end to suffering" is that there's no change. We said earlier that all life is change, so how can the sutra deny change? It denies one sense of change (in terms of past, present, and future) and affirms another (which sees this very moment as being all past, present, and future). What is happening is always just this moment, and in this sense one could say there is no change. Yet saying there is no change does not mean any sort of permanence; it means that just this is happening, independent of all our notions, including that of change.

Life is like a roller-coaster, with lots of ups and downs (sometimes steep ones). When you look at a roller-coaster, it's moving. But at each second, whenever you look at it, there it is. The roller-coaster is life. We take pictures of it, and those are our ideas or concepts. Sometimes we seize on one particular picture and say, "This is the roller-coaster; this is my idea of life." That's one delusion. Another delusion is putting all the snapshots together and saying, "Oh, they are all different. No one picture represents the roller-coaster. Therefore, all there is is change." Then where's the roller-coaster? At any given moment it's there, neither static nor changing. On the other hand, it's not not-static and it's not not-changing. It's just what is, as it is, independent of all our notions.

Over and over this sutra hammers away at our concepts of what life is, trying to clear them away so that we may see and experience our life directly.

"No end to suffering" means there is no escape from being hit on the head, having cancer, being in tremendous pain, or dying. We are enlightened and we have tremendous pain. We're enlightened and we die. Is there an end to children starving, to children being killed? No! Let's look again at the example of the mother and child. When a baby is newborn, mother and child are one being. When the child starts crying, the mother immediately picks up the child, there is no separation. Is there therefore no suffering? No, but in that One Body state, the mother does not complain, she just responds. No separation does not mean no suffering; it does mean no complaining. And in fact, isn't much of what we mean by suffering nothing more than complaining, or taking things personally or egocentrically?

"No path" means there is no path because *this* is the path. Each of us *is* the path. Nonetheless, we must walk the path to realize we are already on it. And that's why we meet in this book: In accordance with karmic circumstances, we have reached the point when we want to study together. Nothing happens by accident. *Because* we are the Way, we have to find it and walk it; because we are the Buddha, we practice. We don't practice to become enlightened, just as we don't go to school to get a degree and we don't do koan study in order to finish all the koans in the system. The realization of any koan is the total realization of the Enlightened Way. Similarly, working on any koan is the total manifestation of the Enlightened Way. Doing zazen with your mind completely scattered is just as much the complete actualization of the Enlightened

Way as doing zazen in concentrated, deep samadhi. And that's because at every moment we are the actualization of the Enlightened Way.

All this teaching is condensed into A, the first syllable of the sutra ("Avalokitesvara Bodhisattva . . ."). At the moment of being nothing but A, everything without exception is right there, nothing is excluded. This is what Shakyamuni Buddha meant when he said that above and below the heavens, throughout the whole universe, "I alone am." That "I" contains everything; that "I" is this A. Nothing is left out or excluded. All is One Body.

When I say that this present moment includes all past, present, and future, it's important to remember that this present moment itself does not exist, it too is just another notion. Every idea we have binds and restricts us. When we let go of all our ideas, we see there are no inherent limitations. That's what is so wonderful! We say that we are limited in such and such ways—for example, we can't fly. But these are notions, nothing more. If I can see life as One Body, that this is all one thing, then of course I can fly. I can do anything because I am everything. And I am doing it all right now! I am flying. I am circling the earth, circling Mars, creating stars. If I say I can't fly, all that really means is that my concept of "I" can't fly. Because my idea of me is this limited, bound self, I don't see that I am one with the eagle. As a boundless, unlimited being, I can certainly fly.

My concept of this present moment also limits me if I become attached to it. Get rid of this notion, too. Getting rid of notions means not being bound by them. For example, remember the snapshots of the roller-coaster. Getting rid of the snapshots does not mean that we literally throw them away, but that they don't limit us, that we don't fall into the trap of thinking any or all of these snapshots *are* the roller-coaster.

Snapshots are snapshots, that's all. They're not life! Similarly, getting rid of the notion of the present moment does not mean not having this notion. If getting rid of notions literally meant eliminating them altogether, I would not know how to get home or open my door or write. The point is that our notion of the present moment is not the moment as it is, it's just a notion. At the same time, this notion is quite useful. In general, we can say this: Seeing notions for what they are, use them as devices; don't be used by them. We're used by them when we cling or are attached to them.

This identification with notions is particularly troublesome when it comes to finding out who or what we are, for we tend to think that we are our notions of who or what we are. When we let go of these notions, we directly realize that we don't know who or what we are at all, and this state of not-knowing is who or what we are!

Not-knowing expresses the essence of our sitting practice. The Sixth Patriarch, Hui-neng, said: "To sit means to gain absolute freedom and to be mentally unperturbed in all outward circumstances, be they good or otherwise."[1] In other words, sitting is just letting what comes up come up, then letting it fall away again, neither playing with thoughts nor trying to eliminate them. The very attempt to eliminate them would just be another form of conceptualization. Let them come up and let them go. We have many devices to help us do this, or rather to help us let this happen. You can concentrate on your breathing, on the letter *A* or the word *mu*, on anything. Concentrating on one thing eventually develops the samadhi of no-separation. Without such concentration, it's almost impossible not to be

1. A. F. Price and Wong Mou-lam, trans., *The Diamond Sutra and the Sutra of Hui-Neng* (Boston, Mass.: Shambhala Publications, 1990), 98–99.

distracted by thoughts and concepts. Once concentration is developed, you find that you're not bound by concepts anymore.

Again, this does not mean trying to block the arising of ideas or concepts, that's impossible! The brain thinks; that's simply the way it functions. Not only is there nothing wrong with it, it's a wonderful thing! The eye sees, the ear hears, the brain thinks. But don't play with thoughts. Thoughts are only thoughts, bubbles, nothing special, as we say in Zen.

We tend to think there's something quite special about strong feelings or emotions, and in a way there is. But the basic teaching of the *Heart Sutra* is that everything as it is, without exception, including special feelings and emotions, is empty. Emptiness is anger and love. Under certain circumstances anger arises in me. The circumstances change, the anger disappears, and love appears. Then a new idea comes up—"How am I going to make some money?" or "It's time to go home"— and a new feeling comes up. Since all this is empty, whatever arises falls away. Nothing special. In sitting practice, we just allow that arising and falling away of thoughts and feelings to happen without attaching to them. Things come up and then fall away; just see them as the normal flow of life.

What stands in the way of realizing this is our strong attachment to our likes and dislikes, which feeds our powerful convictions of right and wrong, good and bad. The fact that I like something does not mean that it's good or right, any more than my dislike of something means that it's bad or wrong. I like something, I dislike something: nothing special. Our likes and dislikes are expressions of karma, and karma too is empty. It can change at any moment. There is nothing intrinsically true, significant, or meaningful about liking or disliking, they have no substance. At this moment, for such and such reasons, I happen to like this and dislike that. There's nothing wrong with that, it may even be wonderful, but so what? We tend to think there must be something basically or inherently true about our likes and dislikes, that others should share them, and that we're going to have them forever. Yet if I like brunettes more than blondes, all that follows is that I like brunettes more than blondes!

People often ask, why do Zen practice at all? The most profound and real answer, I think, is that we do Zen practice because we're enlightened. If we can accept this, all other reasons are beside the point. There will be different reasons for each person, but ultimately I don't think you can find good reasons at all. It's like understanding karma, which involves being able to see the whole picture, all of life. Because this is One Body, trying to understand why any of us is doing anything implies that we have to understand everything. We have to see how the flowers are affecting us, how people in sanitariums are affecting us, how a flood in China is affecting us. Therapy stresses the things that happened to us in our childhood, but karma is a lot broader than that.

When we don't see the whole picture, we think we can narrow things down and come up with some sort of definitive or "true" causal explanation. For example, I could say that the reason I started Zen practice is that in 1958 I read a book by Huston Smith called *The Religions of Man*. The one page on Zen somehow made me feel that Zen would be my life and after that I started formal practice. That's a direct cause, but is it really why I practice? Next I might mention that I met a teacher who exemplified something important for me, which caused me to want to study under him. But broadly speaking, I began Zen practice. I don't know why.

Because this is One Body, a single minute of zazen, of letting go, of clarity, affects the entire universe—all space and all time; past, present, and future. That's how important it is. As

Shakyamuni Buddha said when he became enlightened, "All things without exception are enlightened." You are intrinsically enlightened, but when you experience enlightenment, all things experience enlightenment at that moment. When you reduce your own chaos, you reduce everyone's and everything's chaos. Do you know what this means? Can you even envision what it means to affect everything at this moment, for all time to come, and for all time that has been? Whether we practice or not, whether we realize the Way or not, that's what we are doing. So doing it in the best way we can, in the clearest way we can, in the most enlightened way we can, is essential. Because we are enlightened, we have to do it. There is no choice!

6
Transmuting the Three Poisons

. . . no wisdom, and no gain.
No gain—thus bodhisattvas live this prajnaparamita
With no hindrance of mind.
No hindrance, therefore no fear.
Far beyond all such delusion, nirvana is already here.
All past, present, and future buddhas live this prajnaparamita
And attain supreme, perfect enlightenment.

We've been talking about the first part of the *Heart Sutra,*
which discusses the nature of prajna wisdom. The second part
is concerned with the functioning of the bodhisattva—no wisdom and no gain.

We are nothing but prajna wisdom itself, which is the functioning of emptiness, of this as it is. Emptiness is the state of
One Body, the state in which there are no concepts or notions
of what is, just the one thing.

I don't think of my own body as one body; it just is one body.
But suppose I were deluded enough to think of my body as
many different bodies: this arm as one body, this leg as another
body, each of them a different entity with its own ego structure.
We would have to call this way of thinking a delusion, because

we know the body is one. When we truly realize that everything is one body, there is no notion of that either. To have such a notion would be foolish. Imagine walking around saying, "I am one body!" Everyone and everything is just one body.

The functioning of this One Body is what we call prajna wisdom. I don't think about sweating when it gets hot: when it gets hot, I sweat. That's wisdom. I rarely think about breathing; I just breathe. That's wisdom. I don't think much about thinking; I just think. That's wisdom. The function of the brain is to think, as the function of the eye is to see. If my eye becomes blind, the function of that blind eye is not to see. If it's cold and I shiver, that's the function of being cold. And that's wisdom, too. Prajna wisdom is not the accumulation of knowledge of any sort, it's just the function of what is.

. . . no wisdom, and no gain.

Nothing to gain, nothing to lose. If I put a hat on, you might say I gained a hat; I gained something I didn't have before. But because at this moment this is it, there can be no such thing as gain, which is only a notion. If I put a hat on, that's what is right now. It can't be compared to something else, like having no hat on. Conversely, if I sweat, I don't lose water; sweating is just what is.

. . . thus bodhisattvas live this prajnaparamita

We are the bodhisattvas and living this prajnaparamita is the function of prajna wisdom. Prajnaparamita is the only one of the six paramitas mentioned explicitly in the *Heart Sutra*. The first paramita, and in a sense the most important, is called *dana,* or "giving." In the context of practice, this is giving in the sense of letting go: giving up the self, giving up our notions. Give it all away! Give up all concepts. Zazen is a manifestation of giving because it's the state of letting go. If in your sitting you add on more notions, that's not zazen.

The second paramita, *sila,* is usually translated as "precepts" or "discipline," but it really refers to aspects of the enlightened life. The third paramita, *shanti,* is "patience." One of the names of Shakyamuni Buddha is He Who Is Able to Be Patient. This is not so easy. But if you truly see things as they are, you have to be patient. If you see something growing and you want it to grow more quickly, you're clinging to your notion of how things *should* be rather than seeing what is growing as it is. An oak tree grows about an inch a year; it grows just as fast as it grows, no faster, no slower. If you really see that the oak tree grows an inch a year, you take care of it in the best way you can by letting it grow an inch a year. There's no choice! If you want it to grow a foot a year or ten feet a year, you're not seeing the subtle workings of life. You want to change what's happening to conform to your notion of what should be happening.

The fourth paramita is *virya,* or "effort." We have to totally exert ourselves. Such total exertion is just doing, as in "Avalokitesvara Bodhisattva doing deep prajnaparamita . . ." Because he is the embodiment of prajna wisdom and compassion, Avalokitesvara has to practice, he has to exert effort. In response to the question, "Why are we doing all this?" the answer is because we are already on the other shore. Since this is the enlightened state, we have to exert effort.

The next paramita is *samadhi,* "concentration," and the last is prajna. Bodhisattvas live these paramitas "with no hindrance of mind—no hindrance, therefore no fear." Our fears come up because of our created three poisons: greed, anger, and ignorance. The basic poison is ignorance, which means being totally in the dark, not seeing life as it is because of egocentric ideas. Ignorance creates greed by breeding the idea that we are fundamentally lacking something, and this notion of lack is the cause of anger. But if we are the whole universe, what don't we have? What could be lacking? Is it money? Is it love? Is it some quality that some other person has? We are that other person and that other person is us, our functioning. Isn't it wonderful how we can function in so many spheres all at the same time? But if we can't see that this is all one thing, we need everything and can never be satisfied.

If children could only be taught that this is all One Body, they would be far less likely to steal. Why should anyone steal? We *have* everything because we *are* everything. Look at the beautiful parts of us that are the mountains. Do we need them in our living room? Do we have to own them? They are us! The banks have lots of money. Do we need it all? What would we do with it? A long time ago I learned from my teacher that if I would understand the Dharma, I would never be hungry, never have any unsatisfied needs; I would have everything. If I wouldn't understand the Dharma, I would be grabbing and hoarding endlessly and still feel hungry. Give away everything and I won't be a hungry ghost. Try to grab everything and I'll only get hungrier.

If we are rid of the self, the three poisons become transmuted into the three virtues of the bodhisattva. Ignorance becomes the state of total nondiscrimination, so we no longer discriminate between good and bad; instead we deal with what is in the appropriate way. Similarly, anger becomes determination and greed becomes the selfless, compassionate desire of the bodhisattva to help all beings realize the enlightened way.

The other day someone was talking about all his problems and crises and I heard someone else say, "Don't look at things that way. See them as challenges." Problems and crises create anger and frustration; get rid of the self and they are seen as challenges. Determination emerges and you meet the challenges as best you can.

You run out to save the child about to be hit by a truck, knocking her out of the way, and the truck goes by. If the self is present, anger bursts forth: "I almost killed myself trying to save you! What are you doing, playing in the street like that?" Or perhaps you're feeling that the child is yours, and you get angry because your child almost hurt herself. But without the burden of the self, you just run out and save her without any false idea of ownership. This is total determination. When the self interferes there's crisis; when it doesn't, there's immediate action, with no choice but to do the appropriate thing in response to what occurs.

What is appropriate? Appropriate doesn't mean that you know what to do or that you reflect on what's appropriate. Knowing implies separation from the moment and expresses itself in notions and ideas. Doing what is appropriate in the sense intended here is a function of not-knowing. An action is appropriate precisely because the question of appropriateness has no time to come up, because knowing has no time to come up. If my hand is on fire, it doesn't ask what the appropriate action is; the appropriate action just occurs. If I get very hot, I sweat. Why is it not more appropriate to shiver? The question doesn't arise. "Why?" is not appropriate from the perspective of the One Body. Eliminate it whenever it arises and you have the answer!

Appropriateness is not a matter of right or wrong. If the hand of a demented person catches on fire, he might cut it off. Is that right or wrong? According to our conceptual ideas of what should be, it's wrong. That sense of appropriateness derives from separation, from standing apart and judging what's there. That might be valid in the realm of separation and knowing, but I'm talking about appropriateness that is the functioning of no-separation. In that sense, the demented person's action is appropriate whether we like it or not. We can ask why he did that. The answer must be that he had no realization of one body. If we truly realize our body as one body, we can't cut our arm off when it's burning, we can't even be demented. We are only demented when we see things as separate.

When the parent saves the child in a manner free of attachment to the self, free of hindrances, the action leaves no trace; otherwise, the traces of the action linger on and on. You yell at the kid for days and days, then get depressed and guilty. You take it out on your spouse and your other children, perhaps on your employees. There's no end to it.

Once we drop the self, ignorance, anger, and greed become selfless desires because we realize that all of us are One Body. I now have the desire for the whole universe to be enlightened. Why? Because I want me to be enlightened, and I am the whole universe! I no longer function out of my notion of the small self, but rather out of the realization of the big self, which is nothing other than the whole universe.

Far beyond all such delusion . . .

The basic four delusions are divided into two categories, before and after enlightenment. (Delusions in the latter category are referred to as the "delusions of the enlightened ones.") The first delusion is the belief in permanence, that there is an objective or absolute truth. Whether we call it the ego, the self, or the atom and regardless of whether it's a physical, mental, or spiritual element, what we are looking for is some permanent foundation to existence. For the enlightened ones, on the other hand, the first delusion is that everything is impermanent.

The second delusion before enlightenment is that we can find some state of bliss and happiness. The corresponding delusion for the enlightened ones is that existence is suffering.

The third delusion is that "I" exist, that the self is a reality.

The enlightened ones' delusion is that there is no "I," no self, no ego.

The fourth delusion is the belief in purity, that something unstained can be found. The enlightened ones, on the other hand, imagine there is no such thing as purity, that nothing is pure.

The stage or level of enlightenment referred to here is not total, absolute enlightenment. In Buddhist terms, it's the stage of enlightenment associated with *sravakas*, or "voice-hearers." There are many stages or levels of enlightenment. The final state, of course, includes the realization that any concept is a delusion and is completely free of all delusions.

This very place, this very moment is nirvana; the world of samsara is nirvana; the world of delusion is the world of enlightenment. This very body is the enlightened body, is One Body. Not being able to find reality outside, we search inside, but we can't find it there either because reality is everywhere, it's the whole thing. This being the case, where is inside? Where is outside? Earlier I spoke about maha, a term meaning no outside, no inside, and the fact that we're nothing but maha: We are the whole thing. In our practice, however, looking inside for maha works better than looking outside. Go inside and suddenly that path leads to the whole universe.

All past, present, and future buddhas live this prajnaparamita
And attain supreme, perfect enlightenment.

All past, present, and future buddhas are none other than ourselves. But until we experience this, until we can say with the utmost conviction and all our sincerity that we are the enlightened ones, until we live that way, we are not buddhas. (Being Buddha does not mean being aware of yourself as Buddha, as an Enlightened One. If you have this notion, you are not yet awake.) Intrinsically, we are the Enlightened One, we are the Buddha; experientially, we have to become the Buddha (Maitreya Buddha, the one who is waiting to come, to appear). We are the Messiah and we have to realize it. Because we are the supreme, perfect enlightenment, we have to attain the supreme, perfect enlightenment. And that is what we are doing in our practice.

Whether we speak of becoming Maitreya Buddha, or becoming the Messiah, or becoming *anuttara samyaksambodhi* (supreme, perfect enlightenment), it's all the same thing, it's all this very moment. In different religious traditions there are various ways of expressing it, but the importance of this moment is the same. We can consult innumerable books and authorities, all using different terminologies, but the test, as far as I'm concerned, is simply: are we or are we not talking about this moment? There cannot be two completely different realizations of what this moment is. The presentations or descriptions of what this moment is will differ, but if the realizations themselves don't turn out to be the same upon closer inspection, then the people involved can't be talking about this moment. I have spoken with many different representatives of the various spiritual traditions, and I have always found that when we talk directly and sincerely to one another, we are always talking about the same thing, no matter what words are used. Each tradition is another way of appreciating what life is. Isn't this wonderful?

7
Letting Go of Letting Go

Gate, gate, paragate, parasamgate, bodhi svaha!
Gone, gone, have gone, altogether have gone!

As I wrote in Chapter 1, the *Perfection of Great Wisdom Sutra* exists in many different lengths, starting from one hundred thousand lines to the present version of twenty-four lines. Each version is a narrower condensation of the version before it. Some say the one-line mantra that concludes this version— "Gate, gate, paragate, parasamgate, bodhi svaha!"—is the next condensation. Finally, there is the single vowel, *A*, the first syllable of the sutra. And even *A* is unnecessary, for this very moment *is* the Wisdom literature; this very moment *is* the perfection of wisdom.

What is perfection of wisdom? Let's look at some important elements that are the core of our practice as well as our lives. In face-to-face study, a student expresses agony over a relationship that ended two years ago and asks me how to let go. What is letting go? There is a little toy called a Chinese finger-trap: You put two fingers into it, then try to pull them out. But you can't extricate your fingers from the trap by pulling; it's only when you push your fingers further in that the trap releases them. Similarly, we think of letting go as doing something: throwing things away, ending a relationship, getting rid of whatever's bothering us. But that works no better than pulling our fingers in order to extricate them from the trap. We let go by eliminating the separation between us and what we wish to let go of. We *become* it.

Do we let go of anger by saying good-bye or going away? Of course not! That doesn't work. The way to let go of anger is to enter the anger, become the anger rather than separate from it. If you even hold on to the notion of having to let go of it, you're still stuck. In a famous koan, a monk went to Chao-chou Ts'ung-shen and asked, "What shall I do now that I've let go of everything?" Chao-chou said, "Let go of that!" The monk said, "What do you mean, let go of that? I've let go of everything." Chao-chou answered, "Okay, then continue carrying it with you." The monk failed to get the point. *Holding on to letting go is not letting go.*

We don't get rid of anger by trying to get rid of it; the same applies to forgetting the self. To forget the self means to become what is, become what we are. How do we let go of a painful relationship? Become the person we wish to let go of, become the pain itself. We think we're not the person, not the pain, but we are. Eliminate the gap between subject and object and there's no anger, no loss of relationship, no sorrow, no suffering, no observer sitting back and crying, "Poor me!"

The Chinese finger-trap is solved by going further into the trap, by becoming the trap, and the same is true of letting go: Go into it. If you avoid the situation, it only gets worse. Totally be it; that's letting go. Similarly, when we sit, it's not a question of trying to do something. Don't sit there saying, "I have to accomplish this. I have to attain that." Just let go and be what you are, be this very moment. If you are breathing, just be breathing, and you will realize that you're the whole universe, with

nothing outside or external to you. The beautiful mountain—
that's you. Anger, lust, joy, frustration—they're all you; none
are outside. And because there's no outside, there's also no inside; altogether, this is you. This is the meaning of Shakyamuni Buddha's "I alone am!"

Ch'an master Pai-chang Huai-hai lived on top of a very
steep mountain. One day somebody went to him and asked,
"What is the essence of Ch'an?" He said, "I am sitting alone."
Alone means "all one," which means no outside, no inside. Pai-
chang did not function dualistically. Everything is nothing but
me. If you are causing me problems, that's me causing me
problems. If this hand is festering, what do I do? Cut it off?
Try to run away? No, this festering hand is me. How do I take
care of it? If I realize the one body, I do the appropriate thing.
How do we know what is appropriate? We don't know! Since
letting go means letting go of all our concepts, ideas, and notions and dealing with things directly as they are, then how *can*
we know? Knowing is the snapshot, the idea of how things
are; therefore, it's not prajna wisdom. The perfection of wisdom is the functioning of things as they are. We say, "Not-
knowing is most intimate." If we can really see this basic point
of life, we can function with no limitations or restrictions; we
can do everything!

Our ideas and concepts are very useful, but we have to see
that they're models, in the way that the globe is a model of the
Earth. It is not the Earth. If we know the globe is the Earth, if
we're full of ideas and knowledge we think constitute reality,
we'll be shocked time after time when things won't go as we
know they should.

When we're bound by ideas and concepts, it's easy to antici-
pate how we'll act. That's our karma, our propensity to do
things in a certain way. But we can step back and look at that
bondage, examine how we act. When we free ourselves of

those fixed ideas, when we no longer know how we're going to act, therein lies our true freedom. Each moment the circumstances change, freeing us to not know what we are doing. Indeed, we are free *because* we don't know. Doing what's appropriate is the expression of our freedom from notions of what's appropriate. Letting go is the manifestation of the One Body; appropriate action is the manifestation of not-knowing.

If we can truly realize that we're One Body, if we can really appreciate the garden that is us, it's amazing what can be done. The trees wither and the leaves fall off. The fallen leaves rot, enriching the soil. The earthworms crawl around inside and aerate everything. The ladybugs eat the aphids and the aphids eat the leaves. The plants grow; the roots spread out underneath and touch each other. The rivers flow, the sun hits them, and water goes up into the clouds; the clouds fly around, water comes down from as far away as the Himalayas. The mountains form clouds, and the clouds come here. The soil goes deep and the heat rises, so the bugs and rodents flourish. Everything works beautifully together! The flowers don't object to decaying and becoming soil again. The soil doesn't say, "I won't let you have my nutrients. I need them for myself." Instead it says, "Take my nutrients. Take my essence. Grow."

This One Body is what we call emptiness. "Form is precisely emptiness" expresses the fact of One Body. Do you know how many different things are going on in one little bit of soil? Countless things, and no two bits of soil are the same. Each flower is different, each tree is different. Each lives and develops its own perfection. There are buds that will never open; not opening is their perfection. Each thing is different, each is complete and perfect just as it is. The very fact that everything is different makes it One Body. (We think of difference as something opposed to the One Body; instead it's the nature of the One Body.) Form is emptiness. When we see that, when we can see everything as it is—all the distinct, different things composing the One Body—we understand prajna wisdom, the state of nirvana, the state of oneness, the state of enlightenment.

Also, emptiness is form. When we see that this One Body is all the myriad forms, we see that compassion is the functioning of prajna wisdom, we see the state of samsara as nirvana itself. Realizing the emptiness of all forms, realizing the One Body, we leave the world of samsara and enter this world of oneness, of nirvana. Yet eventually we also see that this One Body is all of the myriad forms, and therefore we are no longer trapped in the world of oneness or nirvana. Instead, we can function in the world of duality and see that the worlds of oneness and diversity are exactly the same thing.

In "Form is precisely emptiness, Emptiness precisely form," the vital word is *is*, which refers to the relationship between form and emptiness. Form and emptiness, the relative and the absolute, interpenetrate with no obstruction. Getting stuck in either place—the world of form or the world of emptiness—is a serious problem, because life is nothing but the coming and going between the two. We ourselves are nothing but the constant interpenetrating flow of absolute and relative. That's the essence of the *Heart Sutra*. It emphasizes harmony and community (sangha). With this realization we can't live an isolated life; it's impossible to be small-minded. "Form is precisely emptiness, Emptiness precisely form" is the Buddha, Dharma, and Sangha of Buddhism.

But this insight is also in Judaism: God as the oneness; Torah as the manyness (the phenomena, the teachings, the reality); and Israel as community, sangha, or harmony. There are equivalent expressions in every tradition. Why? Because all traditions talk about the same thing—life as One Body functioning as all its many parts.

Take me, Bernie, or Tetsugen. It's obvious that these names

refer to one body. But at the same time that it's Bernie or one body, it's also all the names of the parts of the one body: fingers, skin, pores, hair, blood, water, guts, intestines, inner and outer organs. I have perhaps four billion hairs, all very different. So many things! And all these many things are the one body, they're Bernie, and Bernie is all these many things. Harmony results from the fact that emptiness and form are the same thing. It's so true that we don't even think about it. After all, we don't conceive of ourselves as either one body or many parts, we simply *are*.

We see Bernie as one body, but somehow we're unable to see the whole universe as one body, and that's because we're trapped in the notion of our separate self. By seeing our true nature we realize the emptiness of all five conditions and are freed of pain. The last line or mantra of the *Heart Sutra* is "*Gate, gate, paragate, parasamgate, bodhi svaha!*" or "Gone, gone, have gone, altogether have gone!" Gone where? Here.

The world of oneness, in which no thing exists, and the world of form, in which every thing is different, are not one, not two. They both describe *this*. At the moment a snake bites a man's leg, what happens? "OW!" In the world of oneness, with no concepts or ideas, there may be a reaction of pain, but no perception that something happened. But in the world of form, which is experienced conceptually, the victim perceives that something happened and is grabbing his leg and screaming. Both are descriptions of the same thing, the same instant. This is the meaning of "Form is precisely emptiness, Emptiness precisely form."

But when the sutra goes on to say, "Thus emptiness is not form," there seems to be a contradiction. "Emptiness is not form" means that emptiness is nothing, emptiness itself is empty. Form is everything, and everything is nothing. Zero is infinity, infinity is zero. Both are the same statement. The whole universe is one thing, and therefore no descriptions apply. All descriptions are made up, as in the various ways in which we categorize the One Body into conceptually manageable pieces. We call this "this" and that "that," but all of it is nonetheless One Body. I call it fingers and hands, but it's One Body. In this One Body, in emptiness, there are no hands, no fingers, no mouth, no lips, no anything, and yet the world of form includes all those things. *Because* there are all these things—not *despite* them—the One Body exists. Because it's One Body, the world of form exists; because the world of form exists, it is One Body.

The absolute is the relative, the relative is the absolute, and both refer to the same thing—this very moment. It doesn't matter whether I want to describe this moment from the standpoint of the absolute, the One Body, or from the standpoint of the relative. It's this! It's life! Imagine trying to figure out the taste of a cup of coffee from some preconceived idea. Just drink!

Letting go is hard because we're very comfortable with our knowledge of how things should be. We're afraid of letting go of that comfort even though this knowing is the source of our suffering, even though we continue banging into walls. Remember—"no hindrance, therefore no fear." The fear comes from hindrance, which comes from ignorance, and the ignorance comes from holding on to our ideas. We let go of the ideas by becoming the moment. Unfortunately, this is not so simple.

As I've said before, the point is not to get rid of knowledge, but to get rid of the notion that knowledge is reality. The Enlightened Way to regard our ideas is to see them as tools. When we're enlightened, when we see the oneness of life, ideas cease to be a problem: The more ideas and knowledge we have, the more compassionate we will be and the better we will be able to function. If we have lots of tools but don't know how to use them (or if instead we are used by them), they are hindrances. When we're no longer bound by them, ideas can enrich the functioning of the enlightened state (somewhat like knowing more languages can facilitate communication). See the One Body, and seeing this, use whatever notions are appropriate to the situation. After all, we function in the world of form, the world of notions. Even the functioning of prajna wisdom takes place in the world of form. So please don't think that knowledge per se is bad. We function in the world of form, both before and after enlightenment.

My teacher, Taizan Maezumi Roshi, once began a talk in Santa Barbara by saying, "Tell me what this room is." Nobody could answer! This is like the koan, "Tell me what my hand is." I remember Hakuun Yasutani Roshi, a famous Japanese Zen master, saying, "If you ask this question of any little child, there's no problem. But ask a group of students, doctors, or anybody else, and they'll wonder what the question means. For example, is it intended in a physiological or philosophical sense."

We must answer this radically simple question—what is this hand?—to penetrate life. The answer is in the question!

The Identity of Relative
and Absolute

The Identity of Relative and Absolute
BY SHIH-T'OU HSI-CH'IEN

The mind of the Great Sage of India
Is intimately conveyed west and east.
Among human beings are wise ones and fools,
In the Way there is no teacher of north and south.
The subtle Source is clear and bright;
The branching streams flow in the dark.
To be attached to things is primordial illusion;
To encounter the absolute is not yet enlightenment.
All spheres, every sense and field, intermingle even as they
    shine alone,
Interacting even as they merge,
Yet keeping their places in expressions of their own.
Forms differ primarily in shape and character
And sounds in harsh or soothing tones.
The dark makes all words one;
The brightness distinguishes good and bad phrases.
The four elements return to their true nature
As a child to its mother.
Fire is hot, water is wet,
Wind moves and the earth is dense.
Eye and form, ear and sound, nose and smell,
Tongue and taste, the sweet and sour:
Each independent of the other

Like leaves that come from the same root.
And though leaves and root must go back to the Source
Both root and leaves have their own uses.
Light is also darkness,
But do not move with it as darkness.
Darkness is light;
Do not see it as light.
Light and darkness are not one, not two,
Like the foot before and the foot behind in walking.
Each thing has its own being
Which is not different from its place and function.
The relative fits the absolute
As a box and its lid.
The absolute meets the relative
Like two arrows that meet in midair.
Hearing this, simply perceive the Source,
Make no criterion.
If you do not see the Way,
You do not see it even as you walk on it.
When you walk the Way you draw no nearer,
Progress no farther.
Who fails to see this
Is mountains and rivers away.
Listen, those who would pierce this subtle matter:
Do not waste your time by night or day!

Printed with permission from the Zen Community of New York.

8
Most Intimate

The Identity of Relative and Absolute

The Identity of Relative and Absolute, or *Sandokai*, was written by Chinese Ch'an master Shih-t'ou Hsi-ch'ien. Born in 700 CE, he used to sit on a big, flat stone and therefore wound up with the name Shih-t'ou, which means stone head. Through his teacher, Master Ch'ing-yüan Hsing-ssu, Shih-t'ou Hsi-ch'ien is the dharma grandson of the Sixth Patriarch of China, Hui-neng.

The Identity of Relative and Absolute was written about the same time as the *Song of Jewel-Mirror Awareness* (*Hokkyozam-mai*), which is ascribed to Shih-t'ou Hsi-ch'ien's dharma great-grandson, Tung-shan Liang-chieh. These two poems comprise the written esoteric teachings of the Japanese Soto sect that have been handed down from teacher to teacher within the Soto lineage as important aspects of Dharma transmission. As such, they are embodiments of the mind of the Enlightened One. Both express and discuss the five relationships between the absolute and the relative. The intricate study of these five relationships has long been considered to be one of the most significant studies in Zen practice. In fact, Hakuin Ekaku, who systematized Zen koans in the eighteenth century, put this study near the end of his koan system to serve as a basic review of koan study.

Henry David Thoreau, in a spirit that I feel is quite relevant to the study of these five relationships or positions, said, "Crack away at these nuts of man's origin, purpose and destiny as long as you can. The very exercise will ennoble you, and you may get something better than the answers you expect." The answers we get from the study of the Five Positions and the study of koans are not really the point of the study. By the time we complete them, we see there are not going to be any new answers. Instead, it's the process of cracking away at the subtleties of these five relationships between absolute and relative that is so intrinsically valuable.

In the title *Sandokai*, the word *san* refers to the realm of differences, the relative. The word *do* is "sameness" or "equality." *Kai* has to do with unifying sameness and difference, and is associated with the image of shaking hands. When we shake hands, are the hands two or one? They are not-one, not-two. Thus, kai is the unifying of absolute and relative seen as two hands shaking. Sandokai is the identity of relative and absolute where identity does not mean literal equivalence, but rather that sameness and difference are not-one, not-two.

Synonyms for the word *san* are Dharma and form (as in the *Heart Sutra*'s "Form is emptiness"). Another synonym is practice, as in Dogen Zenji's statement that practice is enlightenment. Synonyms for the word *do* are Buddha and emptiness. The synonym for *kai* is Sangha, which is also the meaning of the word *is* in "Form is emptiness." Sandokai is therefore the Three Treasures (Buddha, Dharma, and Sangha); it is form is emptiness; it is practice is enlightenment. When we say that kai means sangha in the sense of harmony, we mean the harmonious relationship that exists between these two hands, absolute and relative, when they are clasped as not-one, not-two.

The harmony in question is nothing but the fact that Buddha (emptiness, the absolute) and Dharma (form, the relative) are the same thing. As such, they interpenetrate freely without obstruction.

Kai is a difficult word to translate. What term can we use to express the unification of absolute and relative such that their respective sense of sameness and difference is preserved, yet they are perceived as one unit? I don't know, but I think the point behind the word *kai* is best described by an experiment done by the physicist David Bohm.[1] He took two cylinders and put one inside the other, so the inner cylinder could move freely. The space between the walls of the two cylinders was transparent. He poured a viscous liquid into the cylinders, then dropped ink into the liquid. The ink formed globules when immersed; its presence was thus easily discernible.

When Bohm moved the inner cylinder, the ink drops spread out and dispersed until he could no longer detect their presence. It was as if they had completely disappeared! But when he moved the cylinder back in the other direction, the ink globules reappeared. They had been there all along. Moving the cylinder in one direction made it seem as if the differences had completely disappeared and there was only sameness; moving it in the other direction, the differences reappeared. They had never really disappeared at all.

He did this with a lot of ink spots. Depending on how many times he turned the cylinder backward, he noticed more and more ink spots. They were all there!

Bohm used this experiment as an analogy for what he termed the "unfolding of life." He said that all events—past, present, future—are right here, right now, but their emergence depends on which way things move. Some events mate-

1. David Bohm, *Wholeness and the Implicate Order* (London: Routledge, 1996).

rialize, or unfold, and some don't. But they're basically all there even though we may not actually see them.

I think this experiment provides the closest model for the identity of relative and absolute. When circumstances come together in a certain manner, like the turning of the cylinder, a particular event materializes. But in some form it is always there, whether it materializes or not, whether it unfolds or not. Kai means that the absolute—do—and the relative—san—are so completely unified that we no longer see them as two; yet, depending on circumstances, the distinction between absolute and relative reappears, and we perceive one or the other at a given time. Although absolute and relative are by no means transcended in this unification, the unification is a third thing, a new being. It's Kai.

The mind of the Great Sage of India
Is intimately conveyed west and east.

Ch'an master Shih-t'ou Hsi-ch'ien lived at a time when Taoism flourished (in fact, there's a Taoist document called *Sandokai*, too), and he tried to bring Ch'an and Taoism together. In Taoism, the sage is the archetype of the accomplished hermit. By contrast, in Mahayana Buddhism, the ideal is not the hermit but the bodhisattva, the archetypal social worker who is not primarily concerned with his or her own enlightenment, but with the enlightenment of all beings—not with ascending but with descending the mountain, going into the world to help everyone become enlightened. Part of this bodhisattva ideal is the realization that, precisely because no one is separate from the world, there is actually no real difference between accomplishing one's own enlightenment and that of all beings. In fact, one can't be fully enlightened until and unless the whole universe has realized the Way. Master Shih-t'ou Hsi-ch'ien tried to combine the Taoist and Buddhist ideals by using the same word for both. The Great Sage is the Great Bodhisattva, or the Bodhisattva-Mahasattva. The "Great Sage of India" refers specifically to Shakyamuni Buddha.

Intimacy has a very special meaning and flavor in Zen. It's an intimacy that's closely related to harmony and to the word *kai*. The analogy of the ink spots diffused in the viscous liquid is helpful in understanding this. We speak of the intimacy of the ink and the liquid, an intimacy so intimate that we don't even see or grasp it. What is so much in front of us that we can't see it? Life as it is. Life independent of all our notions is indeed most intimate. Because it's most intimate, we can't see it. But we must see it! It's as if we were wearing glasses and desperately looking for them at the same time. Things as they are are so natural, so obvious, that we can't accept them as they are. We can't even see them; that's why they seem secret to us. But obviously there's nothing secret about them. It's just that what is, as it is, is so close to us, such an intimate part of us, that we don't see it.

"Conveyed" connotes two things at the same time: being transmitted and already existing. When we say something is conveyed or transmitted, we have the feeling of it being sent from here to there. But here it is already existing and always manifesting. "Conveyed" tries to capture both meanings. It's being conveyed right here, right now. The mind of the Great Sage of India is not something that was transmitted from Shakyamuni Buddha to his successor, Mahakasyapa, to his successor, Ananda; it's being transmitted right now, right here, everywhere! What we see and perceive this moment is nothing other than the transmission of the mind of the Great Sage of India. So what's being conveyed? What's being transmitted? The mind of the Great Sage of India is just a synonym for *this*: the trees, clouds, the sky, the sounds of planes and murmuring brooks. These are nothing but Shakyamuni, nothing but me.

We think of the body and mind as being limited objects, but when we talk about the mind of Shakyamuni Buddha we mean something boundless. The Chinese emperor gave Master Shih-t'ou Hsi-ch'ien a posthumous name: it meant "endless." A synonym for this mind of the Great Sage is maha, there's nothing outside it. Whatever you point to, that also is the mind of the Great Sage. It's like the sky. The sky is everywhere, it doesn't end, and it contains everything: birds, clouds, the Andromeda galaxy, acid rain. The sky and all it contains are the mind of the Great Sage. This mind is being intimately conveyed right here, right now, in a manner we can't see or grasp. If we could grasp it, it would be like the sky grasping the fact that birds are flying in it. The sky is so intimate with the clouds, the birds, the planes, and the rain, there is no separation whatsoever. To grasp implies separation. The sky can't do that; we can, and those graspings are our delusions.

Among human beings are wise ones and fools,
In the Way there is no teacher of north and south.

We define *wise* as the quality of someone who works toward realizing the Way, toward raising the mind of enlightenment. But in the world of illusion and delusion, in the world of human beings, we differentiate between wise ones and fools. In the world of dualism and dichotomy, we see the sky as something separate from us. However, in the Way there is no teacher of north and south. When we see life as it is there is no such thing as dualism or dichotomy. For the sky there's no separation. The sky doesn't take things personally. It doesn't look at the bird droppings and say, "Why are you doing this to me?" For the sky there's no north or south—how could there be? The sky would have to set up a conceptual framework that enabled it to distinguish between north and south, between good and bad clouds, correct and incorrect winds. You can see how silly that is!

"No teacher of north and south" also refers to the famous issue of the Northern and Southern schools of Ch'an, which taught the gradual and sudden approaches to enlightenment, respectively. In those days, northern and southern Chinese were like two different beings; northerners especially considered southerners barbaric. When the Sixth Patriarch, who was from the south, went to study with the Fifth Patriarch, who was from the north, the latter asked him, "Where are you from?" And when he told him, the Fifth Patriarch exclaimed, "Oh, southerners do not have buddha-nature!" The Sixth Patriarch is said to have replied, "In the Way there is no north or south."

Both the Northern and Southern schools of Ch'an became very strong. But after the Sixth Patriarch's death, as we see in the *Platform Sutra*, rivalry developed between them. One of Master Shih-t'ou Hsi-ch'ien's concerns was to bring the opposing sides together and point out the ridiculousness of their rivalry.

Such rivalry is a part of human life even within Zen, which aims at the realization of the unity of life. There are always splits, dualisms, and conceptual traps that we fall into. Major Zen teachers keep pointing the way to the inherent unity of such divisions as Soto and Rinzai, practice and enlightenment.

There is a koan that expresses this unity, this intimacy. A government official asked Master Yun-chu Tao-ying, "The World-Honored One, Shakyamuni, had the intimate word and Mahakasyapa never hid it. What is the intimate word of the World-Honored One?" Yun-chu called the official by name, and the official answered, "Yes." Yun-chu said, "Do you understand?" The official said, "No, I don't understand." Yun-chu said, "If you don't understand, the World-Honored One has an intimate word; if you do understand, Mahakasyapa never hid it."

9

Subtle Source, Branching Streams

The subtle Source is clear and bright;
The branching streams flow in the dark.
To be attached to things is primordial illusion;
To encounter the absolute is not yet enlightenment.

These four lines are considered the core of the *Sandokai*. The first two are a couplet, each paralleling the other. What is the "subtle Source"? In some way, it's the first major question we encounter in our practice. Synonyms for subtle Source are the absolute, true self, cosmic self, buddha-nature, or sometimes just the word *mu*. The "branching streams" refer to the relative, phenomenal world. The two lines describe what is from two different perspectives.

"Clear and bright" tells us the Source can't be defiled. In the phenomenal world, we say something is defiled, but in the absolute, things are just what they are. They can't be defiled—in much the same way that the sky can't be defiled or stained by clouds, storms, birds, or even bird shit. We would have to return to the sphere of dualism in order to talk about something being stained or wrong. Someone said that the problem with Job was that he took the whole thing personally! That's our problem as well. The subtle Source is always clear and bright; there's no personality there.

There are numerous allusions to bright and dark in this text and throughout Zen literature. Sometimes light is used to represent the absolute world and dark the relative, as in the lines here, and sometimes it's the opposite. At times, darkness is used to describe the absolute. If we turned out all the lights or went inside a pitch-black cave, there would be no way to make distinctions. It would be like looking for a crow in the dark. The minute we put on the lights, we see distinctions, we see differences. On the other hand, we sometimes talk about light as being the enlightened eye with which one sees the oneness, because it's so bright that all that exists is the light itself. Sometimes darkness represents ignorance.

The important implication of our two lines is that the absolute and the relative are not-one, not-two. The absolute is the relative, the relative is the absolute. Therefore, the subtle Source is also dark, while the branching streams are also clear and bright.

Think of water flowing through these branching streams. We ourselves are mostly water, as is almost everything on our planet. When it rains clouds come by and drop water that goes into the soil out of which food grows. We eat the food, we perspire; the water from our perspiration evaporates and floats back up to the sky. The air becomes charged with water particles, clouds form once more and drift about, until eventually the conditions are right and they drop rain upon the earth again. This beginningless and endless process is the branching streams that flow in the dark, while the flow itself is the subtle Source.

The branching streams are also an allusion to the lineage of Zen teachers. If we think of the lineage as just this flowing, the lineage is not separate from who or what we are. At the same time, while the various streams in the lineage all flow together into one, they are and remain separate and distinct streams. Remember the ink spots in the viscous liquid. Often we have no difficulty seeing the branching streams, but we don't see the Source from which they all flow. Nevertheless, those streams, those phenomena, are nothing other than the subtle Source. The flowing is not separate from what it flows through.

To be attached to things is primordial illusion;
To encounter the absolute is not yet enlightenment.

We purposely use the word *illusion* here rather than *delusion*. For me, delusion refers to someone who is deluded, and hence to the self; illusion does not. But since there is no self, delusion is illusory; delusion is primordial illusion itself. What is delusion? Delusion is being attached to things. Therefore, the very notion that we are attached to something is primordial illusion, or to put it another way, the primordial illusion is that we are deluded in the first place! Because the realization of this very moment is all-inclusive, it includes the primordial illusion that we are deluded.

Let us compare the notion of primordial illusion with that of original sin. What is original sin? Some say that eating the apple signifies our fall into the relative sphere, that of seeing and knowing differences. But it's not seeing the differences that constitutes our fall, it's our attachment to separation and knowing, not seeing that the relative world of phenomena is the absolute, the subtle Source. That is primordial illusion. On the other hand, if we forget that phenomena exist, we are sticking to the absolute. This is what's being criticized in the line "To encounter the absolute is not yet enlightenment." Since the relative is the absolute, sticking to the absolute is sticking to the relative, which is primordial illusion. Sticking to either the absolute or relative is original sin. It's the sticking, or the attachment, that is the "sin," not what one sticks to.

The point is we have to bite the apple. We can't remain in the sphere of oneness where we don't see the branching streams, the differences of the phenomenal world. We can't be like the sky, that's not our role. Nor can we remain attached to the phenomenal world. The problem is always that we stick to one side or the other, to the absolute or the relative.

We say this poetically by saying that at first, mountains are mountains and rivers are rivers. That is, in the beginning of our practice all we are conscious of is the phenomenal world; everything seems characterized by difference. Then we practice more and grasp the unity of life. All of a sudden mountains are no longer mountains and rivers are no longer rivers; there is just the One Body, just the oneness. In the realization of the One Body, all concepts are gone. But immediately afterwards our brain starts to define and categorize the experience, and we say, "I have experienced the oneness of life," which is another notion. So we say we have to keep on going and see that the notion of oneness is just that—a notion. If we go further, we see that mountains are mountains and rivers are rivers again, but no longer in the relative sense (as in the first stage prior to realization), but in a sense that goes beyond both relative and absolute. Not transcending both, just the dropping away of both relative and absolute as notions.

This also applies to the enlightenment experience. Encountering the absolute is not yet enlightenment. If we have an enlightenment experience, no matter how shallow or deep, if we think that is enlightenment, we're wrong. This very state is the enlightened state. The realization experience, when we have it, is also the enlightened state. The minute we think about it, the minute we call it enlightenment, we're off. Eventually we drop all these labels and just see things as they are. We become completely intimate with what is, as it is, just like a fish swimming in water. Being one with the water, the fish doesn't think in terms of being either wet or dry or even of swimming in water. From the beginning we are intrinsically the enlightened state.

At the same time, the fish *must* realize that it's swimming in water. It's not enough that we are intrinsically the enlightened state, we must realize it. The state of the fish not recognizing that it's in water is also the state of the young, innocent infant, but the point of our practice is not to become a one-day-old baby again. Nor is it to remain a twelve-year-old child who perceives everything as separate from herself. We must see both the relative and the absolute at the same time.

It seems paradoxical to speak of realizing the state of oneness, because that state is one of no-separation, and realization seems to entail separation. But this is actually not the case; it's only conceptually problematic. Being in the state of no-separation, we then have to see it without separating from it. That implies making a leap out of the usual dualistic paradigm of how the brain functions into something else. When we can do this, that is called a turning from the world of duality to the world of oneness *while remaining in the world of oneness*. (It's in this context that we speak of "turning words," words that help the student make this leap.) How clearly this is perceived without falling into either the sphere of oneness or the sphere of duality is an index, so to speak, of how deep the particular experience is.

"To be attached to things is primordial illusion" implies that it's not the awareness itself that is the problem, but the clinging to it. For example, I cling to the feeling that I am separate from others and am thus unable to accept the fact that I *am* the others (and vice versa). We have to be able to see both relative and absolute at the same time and to live and function freely in both spheres simultaneously. That is freedom. Sticking to either side is illusion and bondage. At the same time, however, our practice requires that we stick to one side or the other in order to experience it. Having done that, we must unstick ourselves by letting go of the realization, but we must first have the realization. Just living in the state of oneness without actually experiencing it, is not enough. The fish that hasn't yet realized it's swimming in water is a potential Buddha. A potential Buddha is still a Buddha, of course, but only a potential one. A child of the Buddha is a Buddha and, at the same time, a child. The child has to grow up. And there is no way not to grow up!

10

Intermingle Even as They Shine Alone

All spheres, every sense and field, intermingle even as they
  shine alone,
Interacting even as they merge,
Yet keeping their places in expressions of their own.

In its original version, the *Sandokai* uses the word *mon* for
"sense," which also means "gate." In other words, the things
that pass through these gates are the objects of the various
senses. There are six senses, the sixth being the brain. But this
metaphor of gates also refers to what we fundamentally are,
for we are nothing but these gates.

This is expressed in the well-known koan dealing with
these gates as true nature: A monk asked Ch'an Master Chao-
chou Ts'ung-shen, "What is the essence of Zen?" Chao-chou
replied, "East-gate, West-gate, North-gate, South-gate." The
town of Chao-chou (from which Master Chao-chou's name
derives) was surrounded by a wall with four gates. Superfi-
cially, Chao-chou was saying that one could enter the town
from any direction. More important, he was saying that he
himself—and all of us—was nothing but these four gates
through which phenomena come and go incessantly. It's not

that we have these senses—we *are* nothing but these gates, these senses. Being so, we are no-thing, no-self; this is true nature. Ch'an Master Lin-chi I-hsüan, founder of Rinzai Zen, expressed this as follows: "Here in this lump of flesh there is a True Man with no rank. Constantly he goes in and out the gates of your face. If there are any of you who don't know this for a fact, then look! Look!"[1]

How do senses and fields intermingle even as they shine alone? The original line is *ego to fu ego to*. *Ego* means "to mutually go round and round each other"; *fu* is "negation"; and *to* is the conjunction "and." So sense-objects (everything that comes in through our senses, including thoughts) mutually go round and round each other, and at the same time they don't. They intermingle, interpenetrate, and are interdependent on the one hand; simultaneously, they're completely independent—they shine alone—on the other hand.

Think again of the ink spots in the viscous fluid. When you move the cylinder, the ink drop merges with the fluid in such a way that it's no longer visible as a separate ink drop; move the cylinder in the other direction and the ink drop reappears. Even though the ink merges with the fluid, it doesn't lose its distinct individuality. At the same time, such individuality can't be separated from the fluid. The individuality of the ink drop is retained in the sense that it's there and not there at the same time, manifesting in accordance with appropriate circumstances.

Take the case of the eye, for example. Conceptually, we can distinguish various things: the eye, the sense of sight, the objects of sight (particular images); all of these are like ink drops. Their intermingling is what we call "seeing," that's the viscous liquid. The seeing is what is seen (and vice versa).

1. Burton Watson, trans., *The Zen Teachings of Master Lin-chi* (Boston, Mass.: Shambhala Publications, 1993), 13.

Interacting even as they merge
Yet keeping their places in expressions of their own.

The first line expresses the boundless manner in which part and whole interpenetrate. Any phenomenon, no matter what it is, affects everything else in the whole universe and is in turn affected by everything in the universe. At the same time, "keeping their places in expressions of their own" emphasizes that this all-inclusive merging of phenomena does not in any way imply a loss of distinctness or individuality.

Dogen Zenji says in *Genjokoan*:

> Gaining enlightenment is like the moon reflecting
> in the water.
> The moon does not get wet, nor is the water
> disturbed. Although its light is extensive
> and great, the moon is reflected even in a puddle an inch
>   across.
> The whole moon and the whole sky are reflected in
> the dewdrop in the grass, in one drop of
> water. Enlightenment does not disturb the
> person, just as the moon does not disturb
> the water.
> A person does not hinder enlightenment, just as
> the dewdrop does not hinder the moon.
> The depth of the drop is the height of the moon.[2]

Thus, the distinctness of phenomena is not disturbed by their merging into one, nor is this merging hindered by the fact that their distinctness is retained.

2. *The Way of Everyday Life: Zen Master Dogen's Genjokoan with Commentary by Hakuyu Taizan Maezumi.* (Los Angeles: Center Publications, 1978). Revision by Hakuyu Taizan Maezumi and Frances Dojun Cook of translation by Chotan Aitken Roshi and Kazuaki Tanahashi.

"Keeping their places in expression of their own" has an additional connotation. It refers to the fact that each sense-object is absolute as it is; in that sense all sense-objects are the same. Even the notion of the self is just a sense-object (a thought perceived by the brain, which is the sixth sense). The sameness of all sense-objects is what is meant by *do* in *Sandokai*: Everything—no matter what it is—is just a dharma, just a phenomenon, just an ink-drop appearing, disappearing, and reappearing. This applies to all ideas, concepts, or notions as well (for they are nothing other than sense-objects of the brain). So the notion of a unicorn is just as absolute as the image of an oak tree. Both are dharmas. We may think that the image of the oak tree is real, whereas the notion of the unicorn is unreal, but both are just dharmas, both are nothing but the conditioned result of various interminglings, senses, and objects coming together, or "co-arising."

We each have our own uniqueness; simultaneously, each of us is nothing but the One Body, this one intermingling of dharmas. At the same time that this is One Body, each phenomenon is completely independent and has its own uniqueness. The fact that each dharma is completely independent, unique, and thus absolute in its own right *is* the sameness. But because each phenomenon or dharma is also the One Body, it's nothing special.

In the beginning, I mentioned that this poem is a meticulous study of the five relationships between relative and absolute, often referred to as the Five Positions. The *Heart Sutra* stops after having said that absolute and relative, emptiness and form, are not-one, not-two. The *Sandokai* urges us to go a little further. There are two ways to look at these Five Positions. One looks at them horizontally, as all being on the same level. That means we can look at each moment, each event, from these five different viewpoints. The other looks at them vertically, as making up a chain of progression, with one representing a higher level of practice than the preceding one until we get to the last position, which goes beyond absolute and relative.

In the scheme of the Five Positions, "all spheres, every sense and field" describes the relative alone; "keeping their places in expressions of their own" describes the absolute alone; "intermingle even as they shine alone" describes the absolute within the relative; and "interacting even as they merge" describes the relative within the absolute. Since the absolute is the One Body, anything I isolate within it is not the relative, but the relative within the absolute. We see the ink drop both as an individual ink drop and as completely merged with everything all at the same time. Talking about intermingling even as they shine alone is dualistic talk; so is saying that each dharma is the whole universe.

We haven't yet left the dualistic realm, which is the realm of notions like absolute and relative. Going beyond such notions is the fifth position, no-position. Because absolute and relative are fundamentally a pair, we can go beyond them. This means letting go of them as notions, which in turn entails functioning out of both at the same time, coming now from one, now from the other, depending on what's appropriate to the circumstance and situation.

Forms differ primarily in shape and character
And sounds in harsh or soothing tones.
The dark makes all words one;
The brightness distinguishes good and bad phrases.

Sameness is the fact that everything is unique just as it is. Each and every thing is different. That difference is the only thing we and everything in the world have in common. As human beings, we like to think that there's something we all share. For instance, we often say that all people want the same basic things or care about the same things. But the truth is, we're all different. In fact, the only thing we have in common, the only thing that's the same about us, is that we're different. Our difference is our sameness, and this inseparability of sameness and difference is nothing but the Tao, the Way.

Take, for example, the sense of sight. Seeing as such is always the same, but what we see (the objects) are always different. Seeing (sameness) and what we see (differences) are inseparable, and that inseparability is nothing but seeing itself.

The dark makes all words one;

The dark is realized by letting go of the self. Without the self everything is just what is, existing independently of our notions and distinctions. Becoming seeing itself—independent of subject and object—is just seeing, which is like the sky just becoming the rain—we just see, it just rains. This is becoming the Way.

The brightness distinguishes good and bad phrases.

At the same time that we're just seeing, the relative world is working. At the same time that there are no distinctions, we perceive the "harsh or soothing tones," the "good and bad phrases"; there are the differences.

The four elements return to their true nature
As a child to its mother.
Fire is hot, water is wet,
Wind moves and the earth is dense.

The return intended here is spontaneous and natural. It's not a return *from* something *to* something else. The true nature these elements return to is nothing but the four elements themselves (fire, water, wind, and earth), and the four elements are nothing but their true nature. When we say fire is hot, fire and being hot are not two different things; the same is true for "water is wet, wind moves, and the earth is dense."

True nature has three characteristics: The first is that it's devoid of self, personality, or essence; the second is that nothing can defile it (or purify it); and the third is it's totally free. If we take the vast, empty sky as an image of true nature, the sky is nothing and thus contains or is everything; being everything, it can't be defiled by anything; and being nothing, it's without boundary or attachment.

Eye and form, ear and sound, nose and smell,
Tongue and taste, the sweet and sour:
Each independent of the other
Like leaves that come from the same root.
And though leaves and root must go back to the Source
Both root and leaves have their own uses.

The leaves refer to the relative, the differences, and the root to the absolute, the One Body. The Source to which leaves and root go back is *shu* in Japanese, or "essence." Another synonym is the mind of the Great Sage of India. If we can see the Source, we can see the mind of the Great Sage of India. This Source is the source of this very moment. When we work on a koan such as "What is your original face before your parents were born?" or "What is the sound of one hand?" we are dealing with the root. The Source is prior to that. It's what both the absolute and the relative go back to and derive from.

A big mistake commonly made in studying Zen is to think there's something inherently wrong with the world of duality and that it's to be transcended or somehow discarded once and for all. The point is not to negate or transcend duality, but to totally immerse oneself in it. Totally becoming duality means totally becoming not only the relative but the absolute as well, because the distinction between the two is nothing but a notion. What is the Source then? What is the very state that absolute and relative go back to? Since both absolute and relative function in the world of dualism, we have to go beyond that state and drop the notion of dualism altogether, which means dropping *all* our notions—including those of absolute, relative, and Source. That is the state of not-knowing.

There is an interesting koan about this from the *Mumonkan,* a well-known collection of koans, called "Hsi-chung Makes Carts."[3] Hsi-chung supposedly invented the cart, which in those days had two wheels and an axle. The koan asks, what happens if you take off the two wheels and the axle? The two wheels refer to the world of dualism: one wheel is the absolute and the other the relative; one is the leaves and the other the root. When you take off the two wheels, you're left with the axle, the state of oneness, but take away the axle too (the state of oneness as a concept is still in the realm of dualism) and what's left? The *Sandokai* says that both the axle and the wheels remain—"both root and leaves have their own uses." What remains when all notions have dropped away is just the functioning of everything as it is, independent of our ideas of what they are or should be, now functioning freely because we are no longer bound by notions. In a sense it's confusing even to say that the axle and wheels remain, because they don't go anywhere! In returning to their true nature, their boundlessly free functioning is vividly manifesting right here, right now.

In our daily lives we function in the world of dualism without any self-conscious awareness that we are in the world of dualism. (Like the Molière character, it never occurs to us to

3. Zenkei Shibayama, *The Gateless Barrier: Zen Comments on the Mumonkan* (Boston: Shambhala Publications, 2000), 72.

think that we are speaking prose.) The very notion of dualism is just a notion; it doesn't naturally come up. When self-conscious awareness drops away altogether, we call this functioning ordinary, pointing to the fact that it's completely free of notions, including such exotic ones as absolute, relative, and Source. But we have to resort to expedient means such as notions of absolute, relative, and Source because our functioning is fettered by our attachment to the self. Until we truly forget the self, we have to take our medicine, we have to practice with notions such as relative, absolute, and Source.

But why is it that we have to go this long way around? If "ordinary mind is the Way," as Master Nan-ch'üan P'u-yüan declared, why can't we just be ordinary directly? It seems we have to get sick in order to be completely cured. The study of the Five Positions is a kind of sickness in the sense that it's extra, yet we need to use this study as a tool to penetrate more and more deeply into what life is. We also have to realize that it *is* a tool, it *is* extra, and we are deliberately getting sick in order to cure or immunize ourselves.

The Five Positions are just five different ways of looking at this very moment, but this very moment is independent of these Five Positions. It's just this very moment, as it is, independent of any notions, including those expressed in and by the Five Positions. Talking about this moment in terms of the Five Positions helps prevent us from getting stuck in or attached to any one of them as being the "correct" perspective. It's quite common for us to get trapped into thinking that the way we see this very moment is the way it is. Some people, for example, see everything in terms of the relative, believing there's no such thing as the absolute. Others see everything in terms of the absolute, and still others see everything as an intertwining of both absolute and relative (thereby implicitly denying there's any such thing as the absolute or the relative alone). In koan study, the student is asked to give distinctly different presentations for each of the Five Positions, even though there's really no way to present one of them without including all of them.

Another way of answering the question, "What remains?" is simply to say, "Life just as it is." Life is just seeing things as they are, as a constant flowing and interpenetrating, free from contradiction, boundary, and limit. Our tendency is to deny this flow by hanging on to something we have realized (including, of course, the Five Positions). No matter what the realization is, if one attaches to it, it's definitely not it. It can't be it because everything is always changing. Initial Zen training is designed to help us get certain insights that will enable us to see the One Body as well as the differences, in the hope that we will also let go of these insights in order to go further and deeper.

I am reminded in this regard of one of my favorite koans, "How do you jump from the top of a hundred-foot pole?" Our problem is always how to let go of our realizations so they don't stop us from going further. There's no end to these hundred-foot poles; that is, practice never ends. No matter how high the mountain you climb, there are always higher and higher ones. That's the beauty of Zen practice—there is no end to it, it's never over!

There are four aspects of our practice: raising the bodhi-mind, practice, realization, and letting go of all realizations (nirvana). These four aspects take the form of an ever-opening spiral. Raising the bodhi-mind means raising the aspiration to practice and achieve the Enlightened Way. That implies practice. Out of that practice comes realization, and out of that realization comes the letting go of what has been realized—this is nirvana as far as Zen is concerned. Then the bodhi-mind is raised again, and the whole process begins once more and continues endlessly. Isn't this wonderful?

11

Two Arrows That Meet in Midair

Light is also darkness,
But do not move with it as darkness.
Darkness is light;
Do not see it as light.

For me, the most important word in the *Heart Sutra*'s "Form is precisely emptiness, emptiness precisely form" is the word *is.* Similarly, in "Light is also darkness" and "Darkness is light," *is* means identity, equality, or equals. In other words, the very light is darkness, the very darkness is light. Like the ink drop that both completely merges with the fluid and retains its individuality, this very moment is both the absolute and the relative at one and the same time; light is darkness, darkness is light.

As I said before, in Zen literature it's common to look at light and darkness as mutually interchangeable. Sometimes light is the relative and darkness is the absolute, and sometimes it's the opposite. "Light is also darkness, but do not move with it as darkness" means the relative is also the absolute, but don't mistake the relative for the absolute—even though one is the other. "Darkness is light; Do not see it as light" means the absolute is the relative, but don't see it as the relative.

Light and darkness are not one, not two,
Like the foot before and the foot behind in walking.

This metaphor is like that of the handclasp mentioned earlier: Both are images of no-separation, of two functioning as one.

Each thing has its own being
Which is not different from its place and function.

The eye, for example, is clearly not different from its place and function. There is no entity named eye (a notion) separate from its place and function (just seeing). Each relative thing is the absolute. Since that absolute is the One Body, each relative thing is the whole universe.

The relative fits the absolute
As a box and its lid.

The Chinese were masters at making boxes whose lids could not easily be detected. All one could see was the whole thing— neither box nor lid separately—because the seam between them was imperceptible.

The absolute meets the relative
Like two arrows that meet in midair.

Though relative and absolute have completely merged, they retain their distinctness. Despite the cunning design of the box, we must see both the box and its lid separately, not only their merging into one. We must be able to deal freely with both separately and both as one thing.

These two lines commonly occur as an independent couplet throughout Zen literature. In fact, the box-and-lid image is often used to characterize the skill of a Zen teacher in answering a student's question so seamlessly that there's no space or gap between question and answer (Ch'an Master Yün-men Wen-yen was famous for this). Such a response truly "fits" the question.

Hearing this, simply perceive the Source,
Make no criterion.

The original words, *Mizu kara kiku o rissuru koto nakare*, can be translated as "make no criterion," or they can be rendered as "no criterion can be made." The former expresses the experiential standpoint, warning us against making our own subjective standards criteria of judgment. The latter expresses the intrinsic standpoint: Since this is life as it is, beyond good and evil or right and wrong, no subjective standards, rules, or criteria can be made.

If you do not see the Way,
You do not see it even as you walk on it.
When you walk the Way you draw no nearer,
Progress no farther.

We don't practice to become enlightened; because we're enlightened, we practice. For this reason, there's no way to get closer to, or further away from, the Enlightened Way.

Who fails to see this
Is mountains and rivers away.

The original reads as follows: *Mayote sen ga no ko o hedatsu.* *Mayo,* which we translated before as "illusion," connotes the state of being led astray or lost. If we don't see that this is it, that this moment is the state of enlightenment itself, then we're lost, we've gone astray. Being lost is thinking that we are practicing to become enlightened. That is the master illusion!

Listen, those who would pierce this subtle matter:

"Pierce this subtle matter" is my translation of *sangen*. *San* means "to penetrate." *Gen*—the same *gen* that's in my Dharma name, Tetsugen—refers to the subtleties of life, and thus is very closely related to the intimacy we spoke about earlier. The subtleties or mysteries of life are subtleties or mysteries *because* they are so intimate to us. Ch'an Master Lin-chi I-hsüan emphasized the importance of penetrating the meaning of this word *gen*. "Those who would pierce this subtle matter" can be translated as "those who would pierce this subtlety," or this gen.

Do not waste your time by night or day!

Again, this line could be translated either from the intrinsic or the experiential standpoint. I adopted the experiential standpoint. From this point of view we're being urged to work as hard as we can to accomplish the Way because each moment is the very last moment of our life. From the intrinsic standpoint, however, time can't be wasted. Every moment is the Way, so there's no way to waste it. These perspectives are not contradictory. We have to work as if this is the last moment, our practice requires such urgency. At the same time, we should realize the intrinsic side: This is it—*and* you work hard!

Is it contradictory to say that we shouldn't waste time and that we should make no criterion (as in "Hearing this, simply perceive the Source, Make no criterion.")? Whether time is being wasted or not certainly sounds like a criterion. Nevertheless, experientially we must have subjective standards to help us prioritize our actions and determine what is more important, what is less. My guideline is that if your actions encourage you and others to realize and actualize the Way, you're not wasting time; otherwise, you are. There's a subtle difference between having a subjective standard or guideline and making it a criterion. If I use a subjective standard or guideline not to encourage but to judge others, I've made a criterion. If I just say, "Do zazen," that's not making a criterion. Only if I start judging someone based on that, does it become a criterion.

Zen teachers always resort to certain techniques and procedures, collectively known as *upaya,* or "expedient means," but these aren't criteria because the teachers' intention is not to judge. My own colloquial, operational definition of expedient means is knowing when to stick your foot out to trip a student and when not to. The intention is never to judge, though the student may perceive it this way (which in itself becomes another expedient means I can use with that student). You might think that because we are all intrinsically enlightened expedient means are unnecessary. But we need them because we don't realize that we are enlightened. Expedient means are fundamentally expressions of compassion, which is the functioning of the prajna wisdom of no-separation; such empty wisdom is beyond or prior to judgment.

Like all good Zen teachers, Master Shih-t'ou Hsi-ch'ien concludes his poem by urging us all to do something, not just read his poem and understand it. A good Zen teacher motivates students to do something by stealing from their attachment to notions, by taking away anything that might make them complacent and passive, anything they might try to hold on to as a resting place or as an expectation of some sort. The Zen teacher as skillful thief ideally leaves his students with nothing but a desperate desire to accomplish the Way, to resolve the great matter of life and death right here, right now.

What are you waiting for?

The Bodhisattva Precepts

The Bodhisattva Precepts

THE THREE TREASURES

Be Buddha.
Be Dharma.
Be Sangha.

THE THREE PURE PRECEPTS

Cease from evil.
Do good.
Do good for others.

THE TEN GRAVE PRECEPTS

Nonkilling
Nonstealing
Not being greedy
Not telling lies
Not being ignorant
Not talking about others' errors and faults
Not elevating oneself by blaming others
Not being stingy
Not being angry
Not speaking ill of the Three Treasures

12

The Bodhisattva Precepts

Literal, Subjective, and Intrinsic Perspectives

In both the Rinzai and Soto schools of Zen, detailed study of the precepts comes at the end of formal training. For those doing koan study in the Rinzai school, it might take as long as ten years of steady training before one begins the koans on the precepts (or twenty or thirty years if one's training is not continuous.) Similarly, in the Soto school, detailed precepts study is undertaken when one is near the end of one's formal training.

In my lineage, a detailed examination of the precepts involves the study of the sixteen Bodhisattva Precepts and commentaries on these by Bodhidharma (who brought Buddhism from India to China) and Dogen. The study includes 150 to 200 koans dealing specifically with the precepts as formulated by the twentieth-century Soto teacher, Daiun Harada Roshi.

Even though precepts study comes later rather than earlier in traditional study, we must remember that the precepts are part of the blood and marrow of the Zen monk's training, implicitly there in every aspect of the practice. Monastic life is structured in such a way, in fact, that its daily workings embody these precepts. In addition, Japanese Zen monks would naturally have read a lot about the precepts before formally studying them; the number of Japanese books on the precepts is voluminous!

For this reason, I believe that in the West, where most Zen practitioners are not monastic, we must study and discuss the precepts at the beginning of formal study rather than at the end, and keep coming back to them as our practice matures. Toward the end we can do more formal study, but it's important that these precepts become part of our marrow, part of our essence and our life.

Why is precepts study considered inappropriate during the early stages of one's practice in Japan? The reason is that in the beginning it's hard to see or appreciate the precepts from the intrinsic standpoint, which requires that one have what is called *fundamental wisdom,* or penetrating insight into intrinsic emptiness.

In the time of Shakyamuni Buddha, rules or guidelines governing the actions of the sangha developed in an organic, ad hoc manner in response to certain situations. Usually, for each rule formulated by Shakyamuni Buddha, the concrete situation that responded to the rule was specified as well. For example, in those days cotton was an expensive, luxurious fabric. Mendicant monks were always being invited into the homes of laypeople who wanted to treat them very nicely, and so would go to special pains to get cotton pillows or bedding for them. Since monks were supposed to live a very simple life and not to regard themselves as special beings, Shakyamuni Buddha formulated a rule against the use of cotton. The general purpose of all the rules was to promote the harmony of the sangha.

When these rules were transported from culture to culture over the centuries, however, their context increasingly tended to be forgotten; thus, what started out as relative, situational guidelines ended up as absolute, binding norms. Another thing that happened was a split between the monastic and lay communities. It became common in certain forms of Buddhism for only monks to receive the complete set of precepts, with lay practitioners receiving a much smaller set. Moreover, at different stages of monastic life, the monks would receive different groups of precepts taken from the complete set. At some point in the Zen sect, the transmission to monks of this complete set of precepts was discontinued. What was transmitted instead are what we now call the Bodhisattva Precepts, and these are given to both laypeople and monks.

These sixteen Bodhisattva Precepts differ significantly in spirit and intent from those of the original set of rules developed in the days of Shakyamuni Buddha. Rather than prescribing norms of conduct, they describe the various aspects of who we are fundamentally. For this reason, it's impossible to violate them in essence; in fact, it's meaningless to speak of such violation. Yet when we study them, it seems impossible not to violate them. Both statements are true. What is needed here is a distinction between violating them on the one hand and breaking them on the other.

Take a glass and think of it as the precepts. Every moment we are dirtying, muddying, leaving traces on this glass. Why? Because we are using it! Even if we just leave it where it is without using it, it gets dirty. Violating the precepts is getting the glass dirty; breaking them would be deliberately smashing it. We say that anything short of complete breakdown or suicide is not breaking the precepts but violating them. Anything short of actual self-destruction is a violation we constantly atone for by cleaning the glass.

Let me talk about three ways of looking at the precepts, and in the course of doing so, give you a sense of why we can't violate them even though at each instant we are violating them.

The three are: the literal, the subjective, and the intrinsic (or buddha-nature) perspectives. From the literal perspective, one is simply forbidden to disobey any of the precepts for any reason. No reference to situation or changing circumstance is considered relevant. For example, consider the rule that a monk should not sit or sleep—or even stand—on anything made of cotton. A Theravadin Buddhist monk once visited the Zen Center of Los Angeles. Because he observed this rule we removed everything in the place that had cotton in it, including the cushions and mats we used for meditation. From a literal perspective, what we did was absolutely necessary; there was no reason or excuse for not complying. This spirit of unconditional obligation and compliance is characteristic of the literal perspective. From this viewpoint, each of the sixteen precepts is seen as expressing an absolutely binding commandment.

This is not the case from the subjective and intrinsic perspectives. The subjective perspective has two aspects: compassion, and a more or less intuitive sense of rightness or appropriateness. Since compassion here means the direct functioning of prajna wisdom, this aspect depends on the depth of one's realization, which also underlies one's ability to intuitively determine what is right and wrong relative to a given situation or circumstance. From this perspective, the amount of fuss and bother involved in accommodating the Theravadin monk, such as the fact that all this effort was being made for just one person, along with the fact that cotton is no longer a luxurious item, would all be taken into consideration before any action was taken.

The third perspective is the intrinsic, which expresses the standpoint of the state of emptiness, the realm of oneness. From this standpoint, it's impossible to violate any of the precepts because there simply are no such things as precepts in this realm of oneness (or anything else, for that matter). There are no aspects of life, there is only the One Body of life itself, devoid of any trace of manyness but never the same from one instant to the next. From this perspective, there is no difference between cotton and anything else, no distinction between the luxurious and the nonluxurious. There are simply no distinctions whatsoever.

The point is that we're supposed to maintain the precepts from all three perspectives at the same time; it's not a matter of choosing one over the other. From the intrinsic standpoint, there is no way to violate the precepts; from the literal standpoint, there is almost no way not to violate them. It seems impossible to maintain these three perspectives simultaneously. The only way it can be done is if we can fully be in the state of oneness. When we are in that state, we are just doing, just functioning, and the three perspectives disappear altogether. In fact, the way we clear up violations of the precepts is by "at-one-ment," by being in the state of no-separation.

From the intrinsic standpoint, we say that the sixteen Bodhisattva Precepts may be condensed into the first: Be Buddha, be the Enlightened One, be at-one. This first precept is then expanded to become the Three Treasures:

Be Buddha.
Be Dharma.
Be Sangha.

These Three Treasures are the foundation or manifestation of the source of our life.

Next are the Three Pure Precepts:

Cease from evil.
Do good.
Do good for others.

These are called the Body of the Three Treasures. The Pure Precepts, when expanded, become the Ten Grave Precepts, which are the functioning of the body of the Three Treasures.

The purpose of the study of the precepts is to deepen our awareness of the aspects of our lives and our understanding of why we are making the glass dirty all the time. As a result, we are led in the direction of taking better care of the glass. The reasons for or causes of the glass getting dirty are not necessarily a matter of good or bad, nor are they ultimately as important as cleaning the glass. When we study the precepts, our understanding of—and gratitude for—everything involved in making the glass dirty and clean is deepened and expanded. This is why such an emphasis is placed on cleaning in a Zen monastery. It doesn't matter whether you think anything is dirty or not, just clean! Cleaning is going on constantly. Becoming this process of cleaning, the Zen student is inevitably changed, as are her surroundings and the people she comes into contact with. This process of cleaning goes on from the very beginning, and at the same time things happen that make life a mess again. This is endless. We never get to the point of no longer needing to clean the glass.

This is one of the most important points in the Zen study of the precepts. You wash the dishes and then get a new stack in a little while. It's never over! But realizing this, you do not become passive or paralyzed and just let the dishes pile up. You have to look at the mess that's being created. Moment after moment, circumstances expel us from whatever self-styled order we have created in our minds and make us function in chaos. What do we do? We do!

13

The Three Treasures and the Three Pure Precepts

The first three precepts, which are the Three Treasures, can be translated in several ways. I translate them as:

Be Buddha.
Be Dharma.
Be Sangha.

When my teacher, Taizan Maezumi Roshi, and I worked on translating the Three Treasures for purposes of ceremonies giving the precepts, we wondered whether the crucial word here should be translated as "be," in the imperative form, or "being," in the present participle form. We decided the officiant would say, "Be Buddha, Be Dharma, Be Sangha," and the one receiving the precepts would say, "Being Buddha, Being Dharma, Being Sangha." Other acceptable translations are "paying homage to Buddha" or "taking refuge in Buddha."

From the intrinsic standpoint, the appropriate translation would be "being Buddha"; that is, from the beginning we're nothing but the Enlightened One. We have to discover and experience this, but whether we do or not, essentially it's always the case. From this perspective, you can't not be Buddha. "Be Buddha" reflects the experiential standpoint. We have to realize that we are Buddha. Being Buddha, we have to be Buddha—we have to deepen our realization until we no longer have any notion of being the Enlightened One. Once we experience that state, then "being Buddha" and "be Buddha" come together.

There are three different ways of looking at the Three Treasures. The first is the One Body Three Treasures, reflecting the perspective that we're all one thing that is constantly changing, evolving, and unfolding. For instance, the flower falling from the tree in Los Angeles means we are falling with it and as it. From the perspective of the One Body Three Treasures, Buddha is the world of emptiness. This is not some sort of void, but rather the whole universe; or in mathematical terms, the universal set that contains or is everything. If this universal set is full to overflowing with everything without exception, in what sense is it empty? In the sense that it contains everything *before* we name things this or that, completely independent of all labels, concepts, or categories. Without notions, there is no way to exclude anything from this universal set; this is what makes it universal. To exclude something requires the notion, the knowing, of something being this or that. It's this compulsive interest in knowing that keeps us from realizing that we are the universal set. Being this universal set without separation is not-knowing.

The Dharma of the One Body Three Treasures is the world of forms, phenomena, manyness. It is equivalent to all the possible ways you can classify or conceptualize the members of the universal set. If you look at a mandala, you see an image or model of this universal set: At the center is

Vairochana Buddha, representing the world of emptiness, and spreading out from this center are all the forms that can exist. The center is all possible forms; all possible forms are the center. This is because the center is a point without dimension. Being nothing, it excludes nothing; excluding nothing, it's everything.

The Sangha of the One Body Three Treasures is the harmony that exists between Buddha and Dharma, oneness and manyness, emptiness and form. This harmony is the fact that Buddha and Dharma are the same thing. They are distinct and the same simultaneously. So when we vow to be Buddha, Dharma, and Sangha, we are vowing to be all of this. Intrinsically, there is no way not to be; at the same time, we have to experience and realize this. We can't content ourselves with just saying, "Buddha is who I am, so there's nothing I need to do." We have to realize what these Three Treasures are.

The second way of looking at the Three Treasures is called the Realized (or Manifested) Three Treasures. In this case, Buddha is Shakyamuni Buddha, seen not as the historical figure but as the embodiment of the realization that I am the Enlightened One. Whoever is enlightened is Shakyamuni, the manifestation of this realization. If you have not realized this, then although you can comfortably call yourself Vairochana Buddha (representing intrinsic or original enlightenment), you cannot comfortably call yourself Shakyamuni (the realization of intrinsic enlightenment).

The Dharma of the Realized Three Treasures consists of the teachings of the Enlightened One, which usually refer to the teachings of Shakyamuni Buddha as expressed in the sutras. But in a broader sense, we can also talk about the teachings of any realized person as the Dharma of the Realized

Three Treasures. The Sangha of the Realized Three Treasures comprises the disciples of the Enlightened One who realized the Way—not all of them, just those who realized the Way. So when we take the vow to be Buddha, Dharma, and Sangha, we are vowing to be the realized Buddha, the realized Dharma, and the realized Sangha.

The third way of looking at the Three Treasures is called the Maintained Three Treasures. When we study the Three Treasures from this point of view, we are studying the importance of lineage and Dharma transmission. Even though, strictly speaking, there is nothing to transmit, we have to transmit the Dharma; this is the number-one priority for Zen teachers. The Three Treasures are maintained by continuing the intrinsically unbroken lineage from Shakyamuni Buddha to the present. (The lineage actually goes back to the Seven Buddhas prior to Shakyamuni Buddha—an incalculably long time ago!)

The Buddha of the Maintained Three Treasures refers to all the images, pictures, and forms of the enlightened ones. When you come to the face-to-face study room, the pictures of my teachers are part of what you are vowing to be when you vow to be the Buddha of the Maintained Three Treasures. The Dharma of the Maintained Three Treasures consists of all the *teisho,* or "Zen talks," of a Zen teacher. *Teisho* is a difficult word to translate, because it does not easily fit into any convenient classification. Let's say that a teisho is a talk by an enlightened one. Teishos pull away at our notions instead of adding new ideas to our bag of concepts. The Dharma in this sense includes not just the talks, but also the actions of the enlightened ones. The Sangha of the Maintained Three Treasures refers to all those who vow and practice to realize the Buddha Way.

These Three Treasures are very important, like a steering wheel that keeps us on the right course.

The Three Pure Precepts are:

Cease from evil.
Do good.
Do good for others.

Ceasing from evil emphasizes not increasing the amount of delusion in the world, and thus is essentially a passive way of looking at life. By contrast, doing good emphasizes increasing the amount of clarity in the world and thus is more active. Doing good focuses on what we can do to improve our own situation. Doing good for others activates us in all those spheres that we don't see as being us. The first and second Pure Precepts deal with ourselves and the third with others.

When we speak from the intrinsic point of view, where there is no separation between self and other, the three coalesce.

Every action we do can be viewed from the point of view of the Three Pure Precepts. We can always ask ourselves: Is what I am doing right now evil—or causing me to be more deluded? Is what I am doing right now improving my own situation—is it doing good for me? Is what I am doing now good for others? "Cease from evil" tells me not to do anything that will make the situation more deluded. Is the act I am doing helping me to realize what life is all about? This question comes from the standpoint of "Do good." Is what I am doing helping others to realize what life is all about? This question comes from the standpoint of "Do good for others."

Let's look at the activity of Zen meditation in terms of the Three Pure Precepts. If you look at it as time out from the stresses of daily living, then you are looking at meditation in terms of "Cease from evil." If you look at it in terms of individual therapy—finding peace of mind, tranquility, rest, and so on—you are looking at it in terms of "Do good." However, Zen meditation characteristically emphasizes doing good for others because it progressively breaks down the distinction between self and other. It is the source of a powerful energy that naturally flows out and boundlessly extends to the whole universe. The scope of such energy can't be restricted, you can't stop anywhere. If you do, it's no longer Zen practice, for Zen is a synonym for all of life. Those who seek some kind of sanctuary are implicitly rejecting all of life in favor of a portion of it with which they can be comfortable. We have to be the bodhisattva "doing deep prajnaparamita," which means abandoning any fantasy of rest. When we do Zen meditation, we become aware of a formless center—like the eye of a hurricane—which is extremely calm, and at the same time, a whirlpool of tremendous activity reaching out to everything. The energy of Zen meditation itself naturally takes us beyond "Cease from evil" and "Do good," both of which are within the sphere of self, to the sphere of "Do good for others."

A Chinese poet once asked a Zen teacher, "What is the most important thing in Buddhism?" The teacher replied, "Cease from evil and please do good." The poet said, "Even a three-year-old child can repeat those words." The teacher replied, "Yes, even a three-year-old child can repeat those words; but an eighty-year-old person still finds it hard to do what they say."

It often happens that we do something good for us—because it helps clarify our understanding of what life is—that may not be good for others. One example is leaving our young children to fend for themselves in the early morning so we can go sit in the zendo. We always have to look at what is happening as clearly as we can, knowing at the same time that no matter where we stand, we never see it clearly enough.

Another important conflict has to do with opting to cease from evil without realizing that a passive concern of this sort may very likely violate the other Pure Precepts, which emphasize the importance of doing something, of not just sitting back. What must be stressed is that each action, each decision, must be seen from the standpoint of all three precepts. It's not a matter of choosing one rather than another, the three are simultaneously and implicitly present in any action or decision.

The point is to look at what is happening as clearly as possible, whether we know what to do or not. Complete confidence in our actions and decisions comes only with complete enlightenment, so we can't realistically expect that. Even with complete confidence, we continue to violate the precepts, but the difference is that we see why we are doing so. We see the way in which an act coarises with an intricate set of circumstances and conditions, and how satisfying one or more perspectives violates some other perspective. For this reason, we must be constantly atoning, which does not imply self-castigation. It means, once again, becoming at-one. For this it is absolutely necessary to do zazen, to do deep prajnaparamita.

Doing zazen is seeing the interconnectedness of all life, of the entire One Body. We see the extent to which our zazen and everything we do affect everyone and everything else. Whether we see this or not, however, we should at least accept the fact that this is the case. We must realize that what we call events, people, or objects are just relationships, intersections of phenomena that reflect all other intersections of phenomena. It is this big leap that we must make in our sitting. And we can do so because we are nothing but this leap!

Everything we do, even sleeping in our bedroom alone with the lights out, affects the whole universe. When we really see this, our whole life *has* to change. To realize who or what we are is to realize that we are this One Body. The moment we realize this, everything in the One Body is realized. Then we see how much there is to do because our perspective, initially restricted to the self, is now unrestricted. When you see that you are everything, there is everything to be done! Cleaning the glass is endless, and that very state of endlessly cleaning the glass is the state of the One Body.

14
Nonkilling

I would like to speak about the first of the Ten Grave Precepts, nonkilling. This is sometimes translated as an imperative, such as "do not kill," but in the Japanese word *fusesshō*, *fu* means "non-" so the correct rendering is nonkilling. From the literal perspective, it's "Do not kill!" We shall look at nonkilling from the standpoint of the intrinsic, subjective, and literal perspectives, as well as from the standpoint of the Three Pure Precepts.

From the intrinsic standpoint, the standpoint of the One Body, of buddha-nature, or enlightened nature, nonkilling means nothing is being born and nothing is dying. The very notions of birth and death are extra. Life is just this One Body, constantly changing. We can refer to these changes as birth and death if we wish, but strictly speaking, these notions don't correspond to anything. If something is to be born and die, one of our intersections or relationships would have to have a fixed nature; it would have to be nonempty. We tend to believe in the objective reality of birth and death because we see these intersections as substantial phenomena rather than as intangible relationships. The notion of killing has meaning only when what kills and what is killed have a substantial reality. But from the standpoint of the world of emptiness, there are no separate objects or substances. Therefore, from the intrinsic standpoint, nonkilling means no-thing that kills—and no-thing that is killed; hence nonkilling.

From the subjective standpoint, two criteria are involved: One is compassion, and the other is a relative and completely intuitive sense of rightness. Compassion in the context of nonkilling means encouraging or nurturing life. Pruning a tree, for example, could be seen straightforwardly as killing (a violation of the literal perspective), or as an act necessary to nurture the tree. The same could be said of the removal of cancerous cells, as well as of eating and breathing. The nurturing and fostering of life often involve taking life. Compassion points to this apparent paradox.

"Rightness" is defined by four aspects of judgment: time, place, people involved, and quantity. It's a completely relative and subjective concept. For example, let's apply time, place, people, and quantity to the case of pruning a tree. As in the Biblical statement, "a time for every purpose under heaven," there is a right season for pruning and a wrong season for pruning. As for place, one has to know where to prune. Quantity could refer to how much (or how little) to prune. Cutting the tree down altogether would definitely be too much! As for the people involved, a professional who knows what she's doing is preferable to an amateur who might just hack away at the poor thing.

Obviously, how one puts these four aspects together to form a judgment about what to do can be quite complicated. But once again, the point is not to choose the subjective perspective over the literal or intrinsic perspectives, but rather to remember at all times that we should be maintaining the precept of nonkilling from all three perspectives at the same time. This seems impossible! How can I eat (and thus nurture life) without killing? How can I breathe without killing? Since I can't, how can the literal perspective be maintained? Is it possible to maintain all the perspectives at once?

What naturally tends to happen is that, as our awareness of life increases and deepens, we change in such a way that we are increasingly *minimizing* the destruction of life. For example, you might become a vegetarian rather than a meat eater. Although both involve taking life, there is a difference between eating things that are conscious of being killed and eating things that don't seem to have that consciousness. *Whatever* we eat is a life that has been taken for the purpose of nurturing and fostering life. Maintaining both the literal and subjective standpoints requires the compromise of minimizing the destruction of life, rather than continuing to think in absolute terms of either killing or not killing. Although we cannot not-kill (unless we choose to die), we can minimize it. But the subjective standpoint is inherently a relative one. Each of us will feel very different about what life is or isn't, and therefore what killing is or isn't.

Above all, we have to realize the intrinsic sense of nonkilling, out of which comes a deepening appreciation of all that is required to sustain any given life. We have to see the infinite interdependencies of this One Body, of how many things, moment after moment, are sacrificing themselves so we can continue living. When we have really seen this, we will naturally minimize the amount of sacrifice we require for our life and will probably begin living more simply. Intensified gratitude for this infinite support system will increasingly move us to make the best possible use of all that sacrifice. Even if we don't actually realize this intrinsic standpoint, even if we only accept, believe, or reflect on it seriously, our lives have to change. Even if only the notion of this infinite interpenetration of all dharmas takes root in us, it will become less and less easy to act from the narrow standpoint of the isolated self.

The irony at the heart of Zen practice is that the strongest way to follow the precept of nonkilling is by killing the self. If we can kill—that is, truly forget—the self, we are at that moment the infinite life of the Buddha, and are thus nurturing and fostering life in the fullest, most genuine manner possible. When we kill the self, we eliminate the separation that most threatens life and makes killing possible.

Now let's look at nonkilling through the prism of the Three Pure Precepts. From the standpoint of "Cease from evil," what does nonkilling mean? Don't kill unnecessarily; minimize the amount of life you take. Let's go back to the example of the tree. Ceasing from evil implies that I do nothing to destroy or hurt the tree. But this is tantamount to passively standing around doing nothing, which will end up killing the tree! Nonkilling from the standpoint of "Do good" means actively encouraging and nurturing life. From this point of view, I prune and fertilize it, both of which involve killing. If the tree is being choked by vines, I have to cut those vines away. "Do good for others" in this context means that I examine the infinite number of ways in which the tree interacts with the rest of the environment: the grass, other trees struggling to survive, the birds that nest in it, et cetera. Of course, if we were to follow the literal standpoint of nonkilling, we would not prune anything and, in effect, let the whole thing die. Obviously, it's not so easy to know what to do!

Dogen Zenji has this to say about the Three Pure Precepts and the first Grave Precept:

Ceasing from evil: this is the abiding place of laws and rules of all Buddhas; this is the very source of laws and rules of all Buddhas. Doing good: this is the Dharma of Samyaksambodhi; this is the way of all beings. Doing good for others: this is to transcend the profane and be beyond the holy; this is to liberate oneself and others. . . . Nonkilling: life is nonkilling. The seed of Buddha grows continuously. Maintain the wisdom-life of Buddha, and do not kill life.[1]

The following statement about nonkilling is attributed to Bodhidharma: "The ten Dharma worlds are the body and mind. In the sphere of the everlasting dharma, not nursing a view of extinction is called the Precept of Refraining from Killing." As is always the case in his commentary on the precepts, Bodhidharma is coming from the intrinsic standpoint. "Nursing a view of extinction" means adding to or eliminating from the One Body. Dogen Zenji puts this succinctly by saying, "Life is nonkilling." To think of an exception is to nurse a view of extinction. Moreover, *any* view or notion is a view or notion of extinction, since it's only as a notion or view that things can seem to have a separate or fixed nature in the first place. That's what it means to be dead as far as the constantly changing One Body is concerned.

We have talked about nonkilling from six viewpoints—the literal, the subjective, the intrinsic, and the Three Pure Precepts—exploring how this precept, as well as the other Grave Precepts, is to be maintained from all these perspectives at once. There are obvious examples of situations in which it seems vir-

1. Dogen Zenji, *Kyojukaimon (Instructions on the Precepts).*

tually impossible to maintain all perspectives at once. What shall we say about the mercy killing of an animal or person? What shall we say about killing someone like Hitler? So far, we have talked about the case of pruning trees, which is easier to discuss because there is less emotion involved. Is there a Buddhist code of ethics and morality that can help us know what to do? What sort of moral guidelines can be codified for Zen practice? It is one thing to understand the various perspectives from which to see the precepts; it is quite another to maintain them all in practice. Can this be done?

The problem derives from the apparent incompatibility of the intrinsic and literal standpoints: The former says there is no such thing as killing; the latter insists any taking of life is strictly forbidden under any circumstances. But the problem is actually deeper. Life itself inherently involves death and killing, from which it seems to follow that the literal perspective simply cannot be maintained. Is this the case?

At this point, let's talk again about the notion of nonaction, that is, action without separation, which is in the sphere of the One Body, of emptiness. When we talk about nonaction, we are talking about a state in which, in the midst of action, no action is going on. Something happens only when there is separation; when there is no separation, no-thing happens.

Nonaction is not a passive state; it is not literally "no action." It is in fact the highly active statement of no-separation from what is happening. When we speak of nonaction, we are talking about doing something without separation so that no-thing is done. For example, say a man falls down onto the train tracks and a train is coming. Another person instantly jumps after him to help him up. He doesn't think, he doesn't consider the consequences of his actions, he just jumps. That jump is nonaction. Someone else also jumps, but only after thinking briefly about what he should do or where the train is. This is action. Both seem to be the same, but one is nonaction because it's instantaneous, no-thing is being done; the other is action because there is separation, and something is being done.

Now take the case of an atom bomb exploding and thousands of people being killed. This perception takes place in the relative sphere. Viewed from the standpoint of the One Body, no-thing is happening, for we are not in the sphere of separation between subject and object. If what would conventionally be described as killing can also be described as nonaction, can we thus maintain the literal perspective? If I am one with killing and taking life, is it still killing or taking life? The intrinsic standpoint says-that in such a case no-thing is happening. The literal standpoint, however, does not seem to care whether the action is done with or without separation. So long as death results, killing occurs.

Let me say a bit more about doing something and not doing anything. There is a temptation to interpret "Cease from evil" as not doing anything, because doing something invariably runs the risk of messing things up or making them worse. "Do good," on the other hand, requires that we do something, as does "Do good for others." We have to do something, not just for ourselves, but for everyone and everything.

Usually, any situation we face is a mess, in the sense that there is no clear or obvious way of dealing with it. Life does not allow for simple answers; if it did, we would already have them. There are no utopias! The Bodhisattva Precepts are not clear-cut guidelines for action that somehow magically make everything all right. If they were, we would not need zazen. So what are these precepts for? What good are they?

We all have fantasies about doing things in some so-called right way, but what does that mean? There is really no such thing! As far as Zen practice is concerned, we can only speak of doing things the right way after having realized and actualized this One Body. (Actually, there is no "after"; both realization and actualization continue endlessly and beginninglessly.) Practice helps us to eliminate separation between us and whatever "problem" confronts us, it helps us to "become" the problem. Although this does not mean we will magically always do the right thing, it does mean our functioning is no longer dependent upon conceptualization, it's freer. With such freedom of functioning, it's more likely that we will be able to work things out in an appropriate manner. When there is no separation, there is a sense of no choice: being the situation, you just respond. Moreover, the response is this being-the-situation itself.

To go back to the example of pruning the tree: Being the tree, your decision—which is neither the right one nor the wrong one—is implicit in that intimacy. You don't have to think, your functioning is not blocked by the process of conceptual deliberation. You don't stand apart from it, saying, "Well, I think the tree wants to do such and such, but according to the precepts I should do such and such. Yet I feel such and such. . . ."

Take ourselves as one body. We don't think of ourselves as made up of many limbs and cells and water and blood. We just think of ourselves as this body, this one thing, and respond directly in accordance with circumstances. It's not a matter of knowing what to do, but rather one of *just responding*.

Suppose there is a group of Zen practitioners, all of whom are experts on how to prune trees and all of whom have also eliminated the subject-object distinction. They go into the woods and look at the trees. Even though they are one with the woods and the trees, would they all come to the same decision about what to prune and what not to prune? Unfortunately (or fortunately!), Zen practice will not give us an answer to this or any other question. What it gives us is the practice itself, which is the perpetual opportunity to realize and actualize the Enlightened Way. It gives us no more than this! Even when you get to the state of being the trees, you still will not have any answers. Do you need any?

It's important that these precepts not be looked at as answers, or as possessing some sort of transcendent ethical validity. They don't tell us what to do or how to do it, nor can they. Being nothing but expressions of the One Body, they are dharmas arising in accordance with circumstances, and are thus radically situational. The fantasy that somehow we can transcend situation and circumstance and find out what is absolutely or timelessly right or wrong is just that—a fantasy! We study the precepts to realize and actualize our life. Because the precepts are only aspects of that, we can develop flexible, situational guidelines, but that's all. The spirit of the precepts is the spirit of what our life is. Penetrating this spirit requires above all that we realize the state of oneness. We have seen the importance of doing so with respect to the first Grave Precept of nonkilling, but this is equally true for the others. Seeing what the state of oneness is, we see the interdependency of all life and the extent to which sacrifice is built into the boundless process of nurturing and fostering life.

One practical consequence of this study is that we will tend increasingly to do the appropriate thing in a given situation; not the absolutely "right" thing, but the situationally appropriate thing. This does not mean we will know it's the appropriate thing, because such knowing is possible only if we separate from the situation. The appropriateness in question is precisely the functioning of our not being separate from the situation, and as such is a manifestation of not-knowing. As we continually actualize who and what we are, we have to do the appropriate thing; we do so precisely when we are no longer functioning in terms of notions of appropriate or inappropriate.

The only way to maintain the precepts from all perspectives at once is from the standpoint of the One Body. Not having realized and actualized the One Body, all we can do is continually look at the ways in which we are constantly violating the precepts and learn to appreciate all that is involved in such violation, which naturally occurs even in the case of appropriate action and response. The important point is that these very violations point to the interdependence of life! It is because this is One Body that violations are inevitable; similarly, the violations themselves express and manifest this One Body.

For this reason, the point of the study of the precepts is definitely not to feel self-righteous about one's actions. The point is not virtue in the conventional sense at all. There is no possible resting place of any sort, moral or otherwise. In fact, the notion is incompatible with the spirit of interdependent complexity that is life—life as it is, not as some conceptual fantasy that we sometimes insist it be.

Epilogue

The Rule of the Zen Peacemaker Order

I commit myself to the Three Treasures:

> Oneness, the awakened nature of all beings;
> Diversity, the ocean of wisdom and compassion; and
> Harmony, the interdependence of all creations.

I commit myself to the Three Tenets:

> Not Knowing, thereby giving up fixed ideas about myself
> and the universe;
> Bearing Witness to the joy and suffering of the world; and
> Taking loving action.

I commit myself to the following Ten Precepts:

> Recognizing that I am not separate from all that is. This is
> the precept of Nonkilling.
> Being satisfied with what I have. This is the precept of
> Nonstealing.
> Encountering all creations with respect and dignity. This
> is the precept of Chaste Conduct.

Listening and speaking from the heart. This is the precept of Nonlying.

Cultivating a mind that sees clearly. This is the precept of Not Being Deluded.

Unconditionally accepting what each moment has to offer. This is the precept of Not Talking about Others' Errors and Faults.

Speaking what I perceive to be the truth without guilt or blame. This is the precept of Not Elevating Oneself and Blaming Others.

Using all of the ingredients of my life. This is the precept of Not Being Stingy.

Transforming suffering into wisdom. This is the precept of Not Being Angry.

Honoring my life as an instrument of peacemaking. This is the precept of Not Thinking Ill of the Three Treasures.

I also make the following Four Commitments. I commit myself to:

A culture of nonviolence and reverence for life;

A culture of solidarity and a just economic order;

A culture of tolerance and a life based on truthfulness; and

A culture of equal rights and partnership between men and women.

Of Itself, the Fruit Is Born

Throughout this book—and indeed throughout my life since I began to teach Zen in the late 1960s—I've been saying that our practice is to see the oneness of life, to truly experience the One Body. That's the practice of zazen. That's also the practice of peacemaking.

For more than two decades of work as a Zen activist, I've been asked the same question again and again: What is appropriate action? This was the question my students posed to me years ago at the Zen Community of New York. Almost every time they'd go to work in the different Greyston organizations in Yonkers, they would be confronted by a homeless person who asked them for money. They would discuss it among themselves and with me: What do I do? Do I give her a dollar, five, ten? What happens if I suspect that he's a drug user? Will my giving promote substance abuse, or will it truly be of benefit? How do I know what to do?

Often this happened right after morning zazen. Sometimes it happened right after a weekend Zen retreat. They had practiced hard, and now they had to take action. What was the appropriate action?

I also hear this question from people who never do zazen: business executives who want their companies to make a difference in the world, AIDS activists paralyzed by the AIDS plague in Africa, peacemakers who wonder what to do about war in the Middle East and violence here at home. In various guises, their words usually come down to one question: What do I do?

For me, when you're talking about compassionate action, you're talking about the kai, about precepts. So when I co-founded the Zen Peacemaker Order in 1996 with my wife, Roshi Jishu Holmes, we formulated a Rule of the Order that consisted of the Bodhisattva Precepts, including the Three Treasures and Ten Grave Precepts. But we made certain changes to better help peacemakers answer the question: How do we know what kind of actions to take?

As I said at the end of the last chapter, there is no one right answer to this question. What there is, is a practice, the practice of acting with no-separation, of making peace not out of some doctrine, not out of our heads, but out of the realization of the One Body. To bring this practice more explicitly into the Rule of the Zen Peacemaker Order, I changed the Three Pure Precepts into Three Core Tenets.

In order to describe these tenets, I would like to discuss one of my favorite koans. It's the fourth case in the collection of koans known as the *Gateless Gate*. The main case, the koan itself, is one question: "Why has the Western Barbarian no beard?"[1]

The Western Barbarian refers to Bodhidharma, who brought Buddhism from India to China and is considered the First Patriarch of China. He's a great mythical figure in Zen and appears in a number of tales and koans, the most famous of which is: "What is the meaning of the Patriarch's coming from the West?"[2] This is just another way to ask the question,

1. Koun Yamada, trans., *Gateless Gate* (Los Angeles: Center Publications, 1979), 31.
2. Thomas and J. C. Cleary, trans., *The Blue Cliff Record* (Boulder, Colo.: Shambhala Publications Inc., 1977), 110.

"What is Zen?"

We say that Zen is life. So what is this Zen? What is this life? If Zen is life, what's the point of one teacher traveling from west to east, or of bringing Zen from one country to another? What's being transmitted? These are just some of the questions that arise when we talk about Bodhidharma coming from the West.

Keep in mind that Bodhidharma is not some figure that lived many, many years ago. Bodhidharma is us, all of us. It's our teachers who came from Japan, from China, from Tibet, carrying the torch. It's all of us coming from wherever we came from to the places we are. Why are we here? What are we carrying? What are our teachers carrying? What do we want to receive? What don't we want to receive?

There are a number of ways of working with koans. One is to talk or write about them in order to illustrate something, as I'm doing now. Another, by which I mean actual koan practice, is to *become* the koan. In this case, become the Western Barbarian! Become the beard! Become Bodhidharma! To pass the koan is to experience the state that's being presented, and in this koan that state is being Bodhidharma.

This first state of being brings us to the first Pure Precept, "Cease from evil," of which Dogen Zenji says, "[T]his is the abiding place of laws and rules of all Buddhas. This is the very source of laws and rules of all Buddhas." The koan "Why has the Western Barbarian no beard?" demands that we experience this abiding place, this source. What is that? It's the state of nonduality, the state of not-knowing, of nonseparation.

For example, the pictures we have of Bodhidharma show him with a very definite thick beard. If we're working on the Western Barbarian koan, a typical response may be, "But he *does* have a beard!" By knowing that Bodhidharma has a beard, we've missed the point. The point is not-knowing. It doesn't matter how often we've seen depictions of Bodhi-dharma with a beard, when we approach this koan, or any situation for that matter, we must approach it with the state of not-knowing, no separation from the situation or koan itself.

This abiding place, this state of being, of not-knowing, is a very difficult place to be in. It's the place where we don't know what's right, what's wrong, what's real, what's not real. It's the place of just being, of life itself. This corresponds to the first Core Tenet of the Zen Peacemaker Order: "Not-knowing, thereby giving up fixed ideas about myself and others."

Of the second Pure Precept, "Do good," Dogen Zenji says, "[T]his is the Dharma of Samyaksambodhi [supreme enlightenment]. This is the way of all beings." What is the way of all beings? How many of us can say we are open to the way of all beings? How many of us can say we don't have the answer, the right way? How many of us can say every way that's being presented is the right way?

Over the years, the term *bearing witness* has become very meaningful for me. The Sixth Patriarch, Hui-neng, defined practice as the state of mind in which there is no separation between subject and object, no space between I and thou, you and me, up and down, right or wrong. I call such practice bearing witness, which is the second Core Tenet of the Zen Peacemaker Order. According to this definition, when we do zazen, we bear witness, to the Three Treasures, to the oneness of life. Anything we do without separation or denial—driving a car, cooking breakfast, taking out the garbage—is practice, or bearing witness.

But there's probably no one who bears witness to all of life. Each of us denies something. There are some aspects of my life from which I try to separate, to distance myself. We also become a society that denies certain aspects of itself, such as homelessness, AIDS, racism, and poverty. Zazen and all forms of practice in which there is no separation between subject and object allow us to bear witness to all life as it is, this very moment.

For example, one symptom of separation, of duality, is found in the word *why,* such as in our koan, "Why has the Western Barbarian no beard?" Why? That's the symptom of duality. Why do we wake up at the sound of the alarm clock? Why do we do this, why do we do that? Why do we need rules and regulations? Why do we need forms and practices? Why is grass green? Why?

Eliminate *why* from our lives and we're bearing witness. So in terms of our koan, we're asked to *be* Bodhidharma, be his beard. Feeling the beard, being the beard, we see all the problems: that it's unkempt, that food gets stuck in it, that molds grow in it. Instead of asking why, instead of standing aside and analyzing, thinking or talking about it, we *are* it. That's the practice of bearing witness. The second Tenet of the Zen Peacemaker Order is "Bearing witness to the joy and suffering of the universe."

Think of Shakyamuni Buddha's early life when his father tried to isolate him from suffering, old age, and death. We, too, individually and as a society, try to isolate ourselves from those things, from our collective thick, dirty beard that is uncombed, unwashed, uncared for.

When I bear witness, I open to what is. That's how healing begins. Being Bodhidharma's beard, I learn how to clean it, how to comb it, how to take care of it. I learn how to take care of Bodhidharma. The beard teaches us, as do all the other things we try to deny. If we try to teach them, if we go to a homeless woman to teach her how to live, we're not bearing witness. When we listen to her, she teaches us. What does she teach us? To take action. "Taking loving action" is the third Tenet of the Zen Peacemaker Order.

Loving action is the flowering of zazen, the flowering of bearing witness. The third Pure Precept is "Do good for others," of which Dogen Zenji says, "This is to transcend the profane and to be beyond the holy. This is to liberate oneself and others." Many years ago in Los Angeles, I had an experience in which I saw and felt the suffering of the hungry spirits. I was surrounded by all kinds of suffering beings. Almost immediately, I made a vow to serve them, to feed them. How do we feed them? By transcending the profane and being beyond the holy. The point isn't to make ourselves holy, the point is to serve, to offer, to be the offering.

Of itself, the fruit is born. Out of our zazen, out of our bearing witness, the right action arises. We don't have to worry about what to do, we don't have to worry about what's right or wrong. If we function from the state of not-knowing, if we bear witness, the offering arises, the fruit is born. Isn't that a relief?

"Raising the bodhi-mind, the supreme meal is offered to all the hungry spirits." We recite the liturgy of the *Gate of Sweet Nectar* every day. What is the supreme meal? Raising the bodhi-mind. Who is the supreme meal? We are.